MY FIRST
500 KOREAN WORDS
BOOK 2

MY FIRST 500 KOREAN WORDS · BOOK 2
이야기로 배우는 **한국어 500단어** ②

1판 1쇄 · 1st edition published	2023. 3. 14.
1판 2쇄 · 2nd edition published	2023. 4. 24.

지은이 · Written by	Talk To Me In Korean
책임편집 · Edited by	선경화 Kyung-hwa Sun, 김소희 Sohee Kim, 석다혜 Dahye Seok
디자인 · Designed by	한보람 Boram Han, 이은정 Eunjeong Lee
디자인 총괄 · Designed directed by	선윤아 Yoona Sun
녹음 · Voice Recordings by	Talk To Me In Korean
펴낸곳 · Published by	롱테일북스 Longtail Books
펴낸이 · Publisher	이수영 Su Young Lee
편집 · Copy-edited by	강지희 Jihee Kang
주소 · Address	04033 서울특별시 마포구 양화로 113, 3층(서교동, 순흥빌딩)
	3rd Floor, 113 Yanghwa-ro, Mapo-gu, Seoul, KOREA
이메일 · E-mail	TTMIK@longtailbooks.co.kr
ISBN	979-11-91343-54-0 13710

TTMIK - TALK TO ME IN KOREAN

MY FIRST
500
KOREAN WORDS

BOOK 2

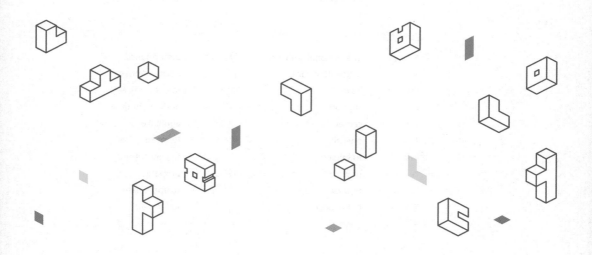

CONTENTS

Day 01   021

외식	eating out
다양하다	to be diverse
마늘	garlic
볶다	to fry
후식	dessert
달콤하다	to be sweet
야경	night view
선약	previous engagement
취소하다	to cancel
훌륭하다	to be great

Day 02   027

비자	visa
발급	issue
해외여행	overseas trip
일정	schedule
일행	group
전통	tradition
체험	hands-on experience
제안하다	to suggest
출국하다	to leave the country
싸다	to pack

Day 03   033

유학생	international student
등록증	registration card
방법	how
지원	support
센터	center
자기	oneself
따라오다	to follow
작성하다	to write
대하다	to treat
감동하다	to be moved

Day 04   039

공연	performance
용돈	pocket money
예매하다	to book a ticket
마침	at the right time
관객	audience
떠들다	to make noise
집중하다	to concentrate
제대로	properly
감상하다	to appreciate
아쉽다	to feel sad

PREFACE

My First 500 Korean Words Book 2 is a vocabulary book for anyone who is looking to expand their Korean vocabulary and learn through effective methods and context, rather than just memorize more words. Our previous book in the series, **My First 500 Korean Words Book 1**, was and still is very popular among beginners, so we have created this sequel for upper-beginner and intermediate learners.

By picking up this book every day and studying each unit, you will find yourself learning new words very quickly and very effectively. In this book, each new word is introduced through a short story, and is accompanied by related words and expressions as well as various types of quizzes.

One of the most important things in learning a language is continuity. The diverse exercises in this book will help you stay motivated to continue studying. Don't give up and keep going!

If you are ready to continue learning, let's get started with this book!

HOW TO USE THIS BOOK

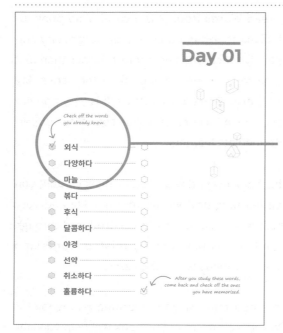

Each "Day" introduces 10 words. First start by checking off the words you already knew prior to this chapter, and then come back to this page to see how many words you memorized by the end of the Day.

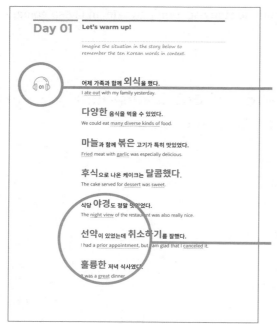

Listen to the words and the story for the "Day" pronounced by native Korean speakers, using our mobile app TTMIK: Audio or by downloading the audio tracks on our website at **https://talktomeinkorean.com/audio.**

Read a short story with its English translation before diving into the vocabulary. This will help put the words, introduced on the following pages, into context.

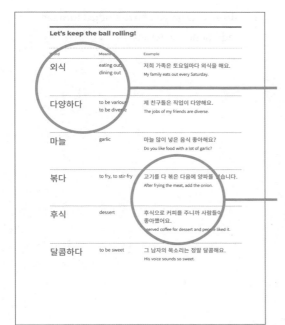

Let's keep the ball rolling!

Word	Meaning	Example
외식	eating out dining out	저희 가족은 토요일마다 외식을 해요. My family eats out every Saturday.
다양하다	to be various to be diverse	제 친구들은 직업이 다양해요. The jobs of my friends are diverse.
마늘	garlic	마늘 많이 넣은 음식 좋아해요? Do you like food with a lot of garlic?
볶다	to fry, to stir-fry	고기를 다 볶은 다음에 양파를 넣습니다. After frying the meat, add the onion.
후식	dessert	후식으로 커피를 주니까 사람들이 좋아했어요. I served coffee for dessert and people liked it.
달콤하다	to be sweet	그 남자의 목소리는 정말 달콤해요. His voice sounds so sweet.

The words are listed here with their meaning in English.

Check out an example sentence for each word. You can learn how and in what context the words are used.

Let's review!

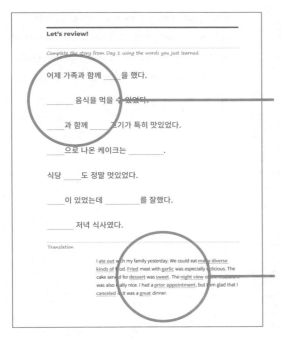

Complete the story from Day 1 using the words you just learned.

어제 가족과 함께 ＿＿＿ 을 했다.

＿＿＿ 음식을 먹을 수 있었다.

＿＿＿과 함께 ＿＿＿고기가 특히 맛있었다.

＿＿＿으로 나온 케이크는 ＿＿＿＿.

식당 ＿＿＿도 정말 멋있었다.

＿＿＿ 이 있었는데 ＿＿＿＿를 잘했다.

＿＿＿ 저녁 식사였다.

Translation

I ate out with my family yesterday. We could eat many diverse kinds of food. Fried meat with garlic was especially delicious. The cake served for dessert was sweet. The night view of the restaurant was also really nice. I had a prior appointment, but I am glad that I canceled it. It was a great dinner.

Complete the story by filling in each blank with a word you have learned, and if necessary, in its correct conjugated form.

Check your understanding of the story with this English translation.

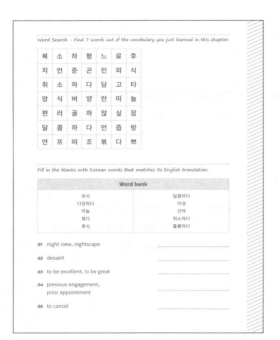

Word Search – Find 7 words out of the vocabulary you just learned in this chapter.

북	소	하	평	느	료	후
치	언	준	곤	민	외	식
취	소	하	다	담	고	타
양	식	버	양	란	마	늘
편	러	골	하	많	싫	잠
달	콤	하	다	언	즙	방
안	프	떠	조	붉	다	쁘

Fill in the blanks with Korean words that matches its English translation.

Word bank	
외식	달콤하다
다양하다	야경
마늘	선약
볶다	취소하다
후식	훌륭하다

01 night view, nightscape   _____

02 dessert   _____

03 to be excellent, to be great   _____

04 previous engagement,
    prior appointment   _____

05 to cancel   _____

Review what you have studied through additional exercises.

QUIZ
DAY 01-10

01 How do you say "garlic" in Korean?
   a. 김치   b. 마늘   c. 차이   d. 소금

02 Write a letter that can fit in all of the blanks. _____

___정	___행	___기
= schedule	= group	= diary

03 Choose a term which is <u>not</u> related to emotions.
   a. 정신없다   b. 아쉽다   c. 따라오다   d. 감동하다

04 What is the antonym of 찬성하다? _____

05 Which of the following does <u>not</u> become a verb if you attach -하다?
   a. 좌석   b. 작성   c. 상상   d. 노력

After you study 10 days' worth of words (or 100 words), there is a quiz covering all of the vocabulary words so that you can check your progress and set new goals.

INTRODUCTION

Grammar Points

The stories and sample sentences in this book are based on grammar points from Talk To Me In Korean curriculum level 3 through level 5. However, in order to make the stories sound more natural, we have used these grammar points from Level 6 and Level 10 as partial exceptions.

Grammar Point	Talk To Me In Korean Curriculum	Meaning	Day
-겠-	Level 6 Lesson 16	honorific suffix	36
-기 쉽다	Level 6 Lesson 25	to be easy to + [verb] / to be easy for + [verb] -ing	44
-기 좋다		to be good to + [verb] / to be good for + [verb] -ing	19
-기 불편하다		to be inconvenient to + [verb] / to be inconvenient for + [verb]-ing	16
-게	Level 10 Lesson 16	an ending that turns a verb into an adverb Ex) 친절하다 → 친절하게	3, 9, 10, 11, 13, 19, 20, 24, 25, 26, 29, 31, 33, 36, 41, 42, 43, 44, 45, 49

Word Meanings One word can have multiple meanings depending on the context. But in this book, for each word, we provide only the specific meaning that was used in the story. This is to avoid unnecessary confusion coming from providing too many diverse definitions for a single word.

Sentence Endings You will see a lot of sentences ending in -(ㄴ/는)다, which is the narrative present tense form. This is usually used in essay-style writing. One exception is Day 36, where colloquial sentence endings such as -아/어/여요 and -(스)ㅂ니다 are used, because the story is narrated by a weather forecaster. However, the example sentences throughout the book are all written in colloquial language.

Parts of Speech This book is a sequel to our beginner-level vocabulary book, My First 500 Korean Words Book 1. The beginner-level book only contained verbs and nouns but this book contains more diverse parts of speech, including nouns, verbs, adverbs, and determiners.

Translations The translation of words used in the story or the example sentences can be different from the provided dictionary definitions. If a direct translation sounds unnatural in the story, a more natural translation is provided instead. For example, in Day 3, the word 자기 is translated as "oneself". However, in the story, it is translated as "him" because it sounds more natural than "oneself".

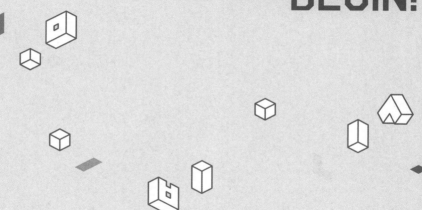

LET'S
BEGIN!

Day 01

Check off the words
you already know.

- ☑ **외식** ------------------- ◌
- ◯ **다양하다** ------------- ◌
- ◯ **마늘** ------------------- ◌
- ◯ **볶다** ------------------- ◌
- ◯ **후식** ------------------- ◌
- ◯ **달콤하다** ------------- ◌
- ◯ **야경** ------------------- ◌
- ◯ **선약** ------------------- ◌
- ◯ **취소하다** ------------- ◌
- ◯ **훌륭하다** ------------- ☑

After you study these words,
come back and check off the ones
you have memorized.

Day 01

Let's warm up!

Imagine the situation in the story below to remember the ten Korean words in context.

어제 가족과 함께 **외식**을 했다.
I <u>ate out</u> with my family yesterday.

다양한 음식을 먹을 수 있었다.
We could eat <u>many diverse kinds of</u> food.

마늘과 함께 **볶은** 고기가 특히 맛있었다.
<u>Fried</u> meat with <u>garlic</u> was especially delicious.

후식으로 나온 케이크는 **달콤했다**.
The cake served for <u>dessert</u> was <u>sweet</u>.

식당 **야경**도 정말 멋있었다.
The <u>night view</u> of the restaurant was also really nice.

선약이 있었는데 **취소하기**를 잘했다.
I had a <u>prior appointment</u>, but I am glad that I <u>canceled</u> it.

훌륭한 저녁 식사였다.
It was a <u>great</u> dinner.

Let's keep the ball rolling!

Word	Meaning	Example
외식	eating out, dining out	저희 가족은 토요일마다 외식을 해요. My family eats out every Saturday.
다양하다	to be various, to be diverse	제 친구들은 직업이 다양해요. The jobs of my friends are diverse.
마늘	garlic	마늘 많이 넣은 음식 좋아해요? Do you like food with a lot of garlic?
볶다	to fry, to stir-fry	고기를 다 볶은 다음에 양파를 넣습니다. After frying the meat, add the onion.
후식	dessert	후식으로 커피를 주니까 사람들이 좋아했어요. I served coffee for dessert and people liked it.
달콤하다	to be sweet	그 남자의 목소리는 정말 달콤해요. His voice sounds so sweet.

야경	night view, nightscape	서울의 야경은 화려하고 아름답습니다. The night view of Seoul is amazing and beautiful.
선약	previous engagement, prior appointment	나는 선약이 있어서 오늘 모임에 못 갈 것 같아. I have a previous engagement, so I don't think I can go to the meeting today.
취소하다	to cancel	오늘 5시에 예약했는데, 취소할 수 있을까요? I made a reservation at 5 o'clock today, can I cancel it?
훌륭하다	to be excellent, to be great	여기 경치가 진짜 훌륭하네요. The view here is really great.

Let's review!

Complete the story from Day 1 using the words you just learned.

어제 가족과 함께 _____을 했다.

_____ 음식을 먹을 수 있었다.

____과 함께 ____ 고기가 특히 맛있었다.

____으로 나온 케이크는 _____.

식당 ____도 정말 멋있었다.

____이 있었는데 _____를 잘했다.

_____ 저녁 식사였다.

Translation

I <u>ate out</u> with my family yesterday. We could eat <u>many diverse kinds of</u> food. <u>Fried</u> meat with <u>garlic</u> was especially delicious. The cake served for <u>dessert</u> was <u>sweet</u>. The <u>night view</u> of the restaurant was also really nice. I had a <u>prior appointment</u>, but I am glad that I <u>canceled</u> it. It was a <u>great</u> dinner.

Word Search – Find 7 words out of the vocabulary you just learned in this chapter.

북	소	하	평	느	료	후
치	언	준	곤	민	외	식
취	소	하	다	담	고	타
앙	식	버	양	란	마	늘
편	러	골	하	많	싶	잠
달	콤	하	다	언	즙	방
안	프	떠	조	볶	다	쁘

Fill in the blanks with Korean words that matches its English translation.

Word bank	
외식	달콤하다
다양하다	야경
마늘	선약
볶다	취소하다
후식	훌륭하다

01 night view, nightscape

_____

02 dessert

_____

03 to be excellent, to be great

_____

04 previous engagement,
     prior appointment

_____

05 to cancel

_____

Day 02

- 비자 ----------------------- ◯
- 발급 ----------------------- ◯
- 해외여행 ------------------- ◯
- 일정 ----------------------- ◯
- 일행 ----------------------- ◯
- 전통 ----------------------- ◯
- 체험 ----------------------- ◯
- 제안하다 ------------------- ◯
- 출국하다 ------------------- ◯
- 싸다 ----------------------- ◯

Day 02   Let's warm up!

Imagine the situation in the story below to
remember the ten Korean words in context.

다음 달에 서울에 가기 위해서 **비자 발급**을 받았다.
To go to Seoul next month, I got my <u>visa</u> <u>issued</u>.

나의 첫 **해외여행**이다.
This is my first <u>overseas trip</u>.

여행을 함께 갈 **일행**도 구했고 **일정**도 정했다.
I also found <u>a group</u> to go on the trip with, and we have also
decided on our <u>itinerary</u>.

나는 일행에게 한국 **전통** 문화 **체험**을 하자고
제안했다.
I <u>suggested</u> to my group that we do some <u>traditional</u> Korean
cultural <u>activities</u>.

출국하는 날까지 시간이 많이 남았지만,
내일부터 짐을 **쌀** 것이다.
There is a lot of time left until I <u>leave the country</u>,
but I will start <u>packing</u> my luggage tomorrow.

정말 재미있을 것 같다!
I think it is going to be a lot of fun!

Let's keep the ball rolling!

Word	Meaning	Example
비자	visa	한국에서 미국 가려면 비자가 있어야 돼요. You need a visa to go to the U.S. from Korea.
발급	issue	신용 카드 잃어버려서 다시 발급받아야 돼. I lost my credit card, so I have to get it issued again.
해외여행	overseas trip	나 해외여행 한 번도 안 가 봤어. I've never traveled abroad.
일정	schedule, itinerary	너무 바빠서 일정을 좀 바꿔야 할 거 같아요. I'm really busy, so I think I'll have to make some changes to my schedule.
일행	party, company, group	일행이 오면 같이 주문할게요. I'll place an order together when my group arrives.
전통	tradition	한복을 입는 것은 한국의 전통이에요. Wearing Hanbok is a Korean tradition.

체험	experience, hands-on experience, activity	저희 학교에서는 토요일마다 체험 활동을 합니다. My school has hands-on activities every Saturday.
제안하다	to suggest, to propose	사장님이 점심시간을 1시로 바꾸자고 제안하셨어요. The boss suggested changing the lunch break to 1 o'clock.
출국하다	to leave the country, to depart	나 다음 주에 출국하니까 그 전에 만나자. I'm leaving the country next week, so let's meet before then.
싸다	to pack	집에 갈 거니까 얼른 가방 싸. We're going home, so hurry up and pack your bags.

Let's review!

Complete the story from Day 2 using the words you just learned.

다음 달에 서울에 가기 위해서 _____ _____을 받았다.

나의 첫 _____이다.

여행을 함께 갈 _____도 구했고 _____도 정했다.

나는 일행에게 한국 _____ 문화 _____을 하자고 _____.

_____ 날까지 시간이 많이 남았지만,
내일부터 짐을 ___ 것이다.

정말 재미있을 것 같다!

Translation

To go to Seoul next month, I got my <u>visa</u> <u>issued</u>. This is my first <u>overseas trip</u>. I also found <u>a group</u> to go on the trip with, and we have also decided on our <u>itinerary</u>. I <u>suggested</u> to my group that we do some <u>traditional</u> Korean cultural <u>activities</u>. There is a lot of time left until I <u>leave the country</u>, but I will start <u>packing</u> my luggage tomorrow. I think it is going to be a lot of fun!

Crossword Puzzle

	01				02
		03			
			04→ 05↓		
06					
			07		

01 issue

02 overseas trip

03 to suggest, to propose

04 party, company, group

05 schedule, itinerary

06 to leave the country, to depart

07 tradition

Fill in the blanks with Korean words that matches its English translation.

Word bank	
비자	전통
발급	체험
해외여행	제안하다
일정	출국하다
일행	싸다

01 to pack

_____

02 visa

_____

03 experience, hands-on experience, activity

_____

04 issue

_____

05 to suggest, to propose

_____

Day 03

Day 03

Let's warm up!

Imagine the situation in the story below to
remember the ten Korean words in context.

나는 한국에 사는 유학생이다.
I am **an international student** living in Korea.

한국에 살기 위해서는 외국인 등록증이 있어야 한다.
To live in Korea, you need to have an alien **registration card**,

그런데 나는 등록증 발급을 받는 방법을 잘 몰랐다.
but I did not know **how** to get a registration card issued.

그래서 유학생 지원 센터에 갔다.
So I went to the international student **support center**.

센터 직원이 자기를 따라오라고 했다.
The center's staff member told me to **follow him**.

그리고 발급 서류를 작성하는 것을 도와줬다.
And he helped me to **fill in** the issuance form.

직원이 나를 친절하게 대해 줘서 나는 감동했다.
The staff **treated** me kindly, so I **was touched**.

Let's keep the ball rolling!

Word	Meaning	Example
유학생	international student, student studying abroad	이탈리아에는 음악을 공부하는 유학생들이 많아요. In Italy, there are many international students studying music.
등록증	registration card, certificate	주민 등록증 좀 보여 주세요. Please show me your resident registration card.
방법	way, method, how	내가 불고기 만드는 방법 알려 줄게. I'll teach you how to cook bulgogi.
지원	support, aid	이 프로젝트가 성공하려면 정부의 지원이 필요합니다. For this project to succeed, we need the government's support.
센터	center	이 스포츠 센터는 오전 6시에 문을 열어요. This sports center opens at 6 a.m.
자기	oneself	그 여자는 자기가 예쁘다고 생각해요. She thinks that she's pretty.

따라오다	to follow, to come with	이쪽으로 따라오시면 제가 안내할게요. If you follow me this way, I'll guide you.
작성하다	to write, to make a document, to fill in	보고서는 다음 주 화요일까지 작성해 주세요. Please write the report by next Tuesday.
대하다	to treat, to face	그 남자가 저를 대하는 태도가 마음에 안 들어요. I don't like the attitude he treats me with.
감동하다	to be moved, to be touched	그 책 읽고 진짜 감동했어요. I was really moved when I read the book.

Let's review!

Complete the story from Day 3 using the words you just learned.

나는 한국에 사는 _____이다.

한국에 살기 위해서는 외국인 _____이 있어야 한다.

그런데 나는 등록증 발급을 받는 _____을 잘 몰랐다.

그래서 유학생 _____ _____에 갔다.

센터 직원이 _____를 _____ 했다.

그리고 발급 서류를 _____ 것을 도와줬다.

직원이 나를 친절하게 _____ 줘서 나는 _____.

Translation

I am **an international student** living in Korea. To live in Korea, you need to have an alien **registration card**, but I did not know **how** to get a registration card issued. So I went to the international student **support** center. The center's staff member told me to **follow** **him**. And he helped me to **fill in** the issuance form. The staff **treated** me kindly, so I **was touched**.

Word Search - Find 7 words out of the vocabulary you just learned in this chapter.

지	원	최	좌	등	할	늦
야	부	방	앞	록	쉬	말
두	머	법	역	증	연	표
감	폰	발	접	션	면	작
동	휴	센	터	쇼	존	성
하	기	거	수	멘	화	하
다	맛	로	따	라	오	다

Fill in the blanks with Korean words that matches its English translation.

Word bank	
유학생	자기
등록증	따라오다
방법	작성하다
지원	대하다
센터	감동하다

01 international student,
student studying abroad

_____

02 oneself

_____

03 to write, to make a document,
to fill in

_____

04 to treat, to face

_____

05 way, method, how

_____

Day 04

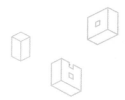

Day 04

Let's warm up!

Imagine the situation in the story below to remember the ten Korean words in context.

나는 **공연** 보는 것을 정말 좋아한다.

I really like to watch **performances**.

용돈을 받으면 바로 표를 **예매한다**.

When I get my **allowance**, I **book a ticket** right away.

마침 내가 좋아하는 공연이 있어서 예매했다.

At the right time, there was a performance that I liked, so I booked a ticket.

공연을 보러 갔는데 어떤 **관객**들이 계속 **떠들었다**.

I went to see the performance and some people in the **audience** kept **talking loudly**.

공연에 **집중할** 수가 없었다.

I could not **concentrate** on the performance.

공연을 **제대로 감상할** 수 없어서 너무 **아쉬웠다**.

I felt so **sad** that I could not **properly** **enjoy** the performance.

Let's keep the ball rolling!

Word	Meaning	Example
공연	performance, show	잠시 후 공연이 시작됩니다. The performance will begin shortly.
용돈	allowance, pocket money	저는 엄마한테 용돈을 받아요. I get pocket money from my mom.
예매하다	to book a ticket	영화표를 예매하려고 했는데, 벌써 다 팔렸네요. I was going to book a movie ticket, but the tickets were already sold out.
마침	at the right time	마침 회사 앞에 택시가 있었어요. At the right time, there was a taxi in front of the company office.
관객	audience	관객들은 모두 일어나서 박수를 쳤습니다. The audience all stood up and applauded.
떠들다	to chat loudly, to make noise	도서관에서는 떠들지 마세요. Don't make loud noises in the library.

| **집중하다** | to concentrate | 1시간 동안 집중해서 공부할 거야. |
| | | I'll concentrate on studying for an hour. |

| **제대로** | properly, right | 어젯밤에 잠을 제대로 못 잤어요. |
| | | I couldn't sleep properly last night. |

| **감상하다** | to watch,
to appreciate,
to enjoy | 저는 그림 감상하는 걸 좋아해요. |
| | | I like to appreciate paintings. |

| **아쉽다** | to feel sad,
to be sorry | 20대가 너무 빨리 지나간 것 같아서
아쉬워. |
| | | I feel sad that my 20s passed by so quickly. |

Let's review!

Complete the story from Day 4 using the words you just learned.

나는 _____ 보는 것을 정말 좋아한다.

_____을 받으면 바로 표를 _____.

_____ 내가 좋아하는 공연이 있어서 예매했다.

공연을 보러 갔는데 어떤 _____들이 계속 _____.

공연에 _____ 수가 없었다.

공연을 _____ _____ 수 없어서 너무 _____.

Translation

I really like to watch **performances**. When I get my **allowance**, I **book a ticket** right away. **At the right time**, there was a performance that I liked, so I booked a ticket. I went to see the performance and some people in the **audience** kept **talking loudly**. I could not **concentrate** on the performance. I felt so **sad** that I could not **properly** **enjoy** the performance.

Crossword Puzzle

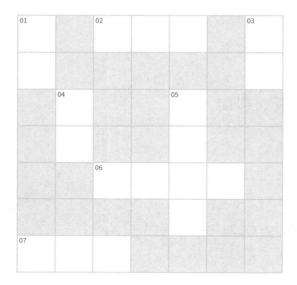

01 performance, show

02 properly, right

03 at the right time

04 audience

05 to book a ticket

06 to concentrate

07 to chat loudly, to make noise

Fill in the blanks with Korean words that matches its English translation.

Word bank	
공연	떠들다
용돈	집중하다
예매하다	제대로
마침	감상하다
관객	아쉽다

01 allowance, pocket money

_____

02 at the right time

_____

03 properly, right

_____

04 to feel sad, to be sorry

_____

05 to watch, to appreciate, to enjoy

_____

Day 05

결정하다 -------------------- ◯

의견 -------------------- ◯

차이 -------------------- ◯

모이다 -------------------- ◯

찬성하다 -------------------- ◯

반대하다 -------------------- ◯

충분히 -------------------- ◯

만족하다 -------------------- ◯

방향 -------------------- ◯

선택하다 -------------------- ◯

Day 05

Let's warm up!

....

*Imagine the situation in the story below to
remember the ten Korean words in context.*

어떤 일을 **결정할** 때 **의견 차이**가 있을 수 있다.

When you **make a decision** on something, there may be
differences of **opinion**.

그럴 때는 함께 **모여서** 회의를 해 보면 좋다.

In that case, it is good to **get together** and have a discussion.

먼저, **찬성하는** 사람들의 의견과 **반대하는**
사람들의 의견을 **충분히** 듣는다.

First of all, hear **enough** of the opinions of people who **agree** and
the opinions of people who **disagree**.

그리고 모두가 **만족할** 수 있는 **방향**을 **선택한다**.

And **choose** a **direction** that everyone can **be satisfied** with.

그러면 더 좋은 결정을 할 수 있다.

Then you can make a better decision.

Let's keep the ball rolling!

Word	Meaning	Example
결정하다	to decide, to make a decision	오늘 저녁에 입을 드레스 결정했어요? Have you decided on a dress to wear tonight?
의견	opinion, view	다른 의견 있으면 알려 주세요. Please let me know if you have any other opinions.
차이	difference, distinction	저는 오빠랑 나이 차이가 많이 나요. I have a big age difference with my older brother.
모이다	to gather, to get together	우리 모여서 사진 좀 찍을까요? Shall we gather and take some pictures?
찬성하다	to agree	나는 현우가 한 말에 찬성해. I agree with what Hyunwoo said.
반대하다	to disagree, to oppose	저는 전쟁에 반대합니다. I'm opposed to war.

| **충분히** | enough, fully | 더울 때는 물을 충분히 마시는 것이 중요해요. |
| | | When it's hot, drinking enough water is important. |

| **만족하다** | to be satisfied | 저는 제가 받는 월급에 만족해요. |
| | | I'm satisfied with the salary I receive. |

| **방향** | direction, way | 저희 집은 서울역이랑 같은 방향이에요. |
| | | My home is in the same direction as Seoul Station. |

| **선택하다** | to choose, to pick | 둘 중에 하나만 선택해. |
| | | Choose only one out of the two. |

Let's review!

Complete the story from Day 5 using the words you just learned.

어떤 일을 _____ 때 ____ _____가 있을 수 있다.

그럴 때는 함께 _____ 회의를 해 보면 좋다.

먼저, _____ 사람들의 의견과 _____ 사람들의
의견을 _____ 듣는다.

그리고 모두가 _____ 수 있는 ____을 _____.

그러면 더 좋은 결정을 할 수 있다.

Translation

When you **make a decision** on something, there may be **differences** of **opinion**. In that case, it is good to **get together** and have a discussion. First of all, hear **enough** of the opinions of people who **agree** and the opinions of people who **disagree**. And **choose** a **direction** that everyone can **be satisfied** with. Then you can make a better decision.

Word Search – Find 7 words out of the vocabulary you just learned in this chapter.

두	추	모	도	충	분	히
화	차	이	중	갑	디	경
토	져	다	기	결	저	초
직	당	깝	차	정	획	운
나	휴	반	대	하	다	국
회	교	출	예	다	역	서
의	견	화	혜	다	방	향

Fill in the blanks with Korean words that matches its English translation.

Word bank	
결정하다	반대하다
의견	충분히
차이	만족하다
모이다	방향
찬성하다	선택하다

01 to agree

_____

02 to choose, to pick

_____

03 direction, way

_____

04 to be satisfied

_____

05 opinion, view

_____

Day 06

Day 06

Let's warm up!

*Imagine the situation in the story below to
remember the ten Korean words in context.*

아이의 **일기**를 봤다. 아이가 일기에 **외롭다고** 썼다.

I saw my kid's <u>diary</u>. She wrote that she was <u>lonely</u> in her diary.

사실 요즘 바빠서 아이와 시간을 보내지 못했다.

<u>Actually</u>, I have been busy these days, so I could not spend time
with my kid.

내가 **가정**에서 **부모**의 **역할**을 잘 못하고 있는 것
같아서 미안했다.

I felt like I was not doing my <u>job</u> well as a <u>parent</u> in my <u>family</u>,
so I felt sorry.

하지만 나는 오늘도 **직장**에 가야 한다.

But today, as usual, I have to go to <u>work</u>.

일도 하고 아이도 **키우는** 것은 어려운 일이다.

It is difficult to work and also <u>raise</u> a child.

그래도 아이와의 **추억**을 만들기 위해서 **노력할** 것이다.

But still, I will <u>make an effort</u> to make <u>fond memories</u> with my kid.

Let's keep the ball rolling!

Word	Meaning	Example
일기	diary, journal	저는 매일 밤 일기를 써요. I write in my diary every night.
외롭다	to be lonely	당신이 외롭지 않기를 바라요. I hope you don't feel lonely.
사실	actually, in fact	사실 나도 벌레를 무서워해. Actually, I'm afraid of bugs, too.
가정	family, home	그 남자는 행복한 가정에서 자랐습니다. He grew up in a happy family.
부모	parents	부모는 항상 자식을 걱정합니다. Parents are always worried about their children.
역할	role, part	물은 우리 몸에서 중요한 역할을 합니다. Water plays an important role in our bodies.

직장	workplace, work, job	제 직장은 서울역 주변에 있어요. My workplace is near Seoul Station.
키우다	to raise, to rear	엄마, 저를 잘 키워 주셔서 감사합니다. Mom, thank you for raising me well.
추억	fond memory	파리에서의 추억을 잊을 수가 없어요. I can't forget my fond memories in Paris.
노력하다	to make an effort, to work hard	꾸준히 노력하면 좋은 결과를 얻을 수 있을 거야. If you keep trying consistently, you'll get good results.

Let's review!

Complete the story from Day 6 using the words you just learned.

아이의 _____를 봤다. 아이가 일기에 _____ 썼다.

_____ 요즘 바빠서 아이와 시간을 보내지 못했다.

내가 _____에서 _____의 _____을 잘 못하고 있는 것 같아서 미안했다.

하지만 나는 오늘도 _____에 가야 한다.

일도 하고 아이도 _____ 것은 어려운 일이다.

그래도 아이와의 _____을 만들기 위해서 _____ 것이다.

Translation

I saw my kid's <u>diary</u>. She wrote that she was <u>lonely</u> in her diary. <u>Actually</u>, I have been busy these days, so I could not spend time with my kid. I felt like I was not doing my <u>job</u> well as a <u>parent</u> in my <u>family</u>, so I felt sorry. But today, as usual, I have to go to <u>work</u>. It is difficult to work and also <u>raise</u> a child. But still, I will <u>make an effort</u> to make <u>fond memories</u> with my kid.

Crossword Puzzle

	01					02	
03		04					
05					06		
	07						

01 diary, journal

02 actually, in fact

03 fond memory

04 workplace, work, job

05 role, part

06 to raise, to rear

07 to make an effort, to work hard

Fill in the blanks with Korean words that matches its English translation.

Word bank	
일기	역할
외롭다	직장
사실	키우다
가정	추억
부모	노력하다

01 to be lonely

_____

02 parents

_____

03 to raise, to rear

_____

04 family, home

_____

05 role, part

_____

Day 07

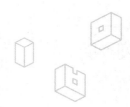

Day 07

Let's warm up!

Imagine the situation in the story below to remember the ten Korean words in context.

지난주에 처음으로 비행기를 타 봤다.

Last week, I took a plane for the first time.

기대했는데 정말 불편했다.

I was **looking forward to** it, but it was really uncomfortable.

먼저 좌석 앞뒤 공간이 좁아서 다리를 펼 수가 없었다.

First, the **space in front of and behind** the **seat** was tight, so I could not **stretch** my legs.

그리고 내 자리에서는 창밖 풍경이 안 보였다.

And from my seat, I could not see the **scenery outside the window**.

답답하고 어지러웠다.

I felt stuffy and **dizzy**.

계속 앉아 있어서 등이 아팠다.

I was seated the whole time, so my **back** hurt.

비행기 안이 건조해서 코도 아팠다.

It was **dry** inside the plane, so my nose also hurt.

앞으로는 비행기 타는 일이 기대되지 않을 것 같다.

From now on, I do not think I will be looking forward to taking a plane.

Let's keep the ball rolling!

Word	Meaning	Example
기대하다	to look forward to, to expect	**이번 경기에서 우리 나라가 승리하기를 기대하겠습니다.** I'm looking forward to our country winning this game.
좌석	seat	**우리 좌석은 앞에서 세 번째 줄이야.** Our seats are in the third row from the front.
앞뒤	in front and back, back and forth	**배가 앞뒤로 흔들려서 무서웠어요.** The boat was rocking back and forth, so I was scared.
공간	space, room	**이쪽 공간에 의자를 놓을 거예요.** I'm going to put a chair in this space.
펴다	to stretch, to straighten	**어깨를 펴고 바른 자세로 앉으세요.** Straighten your shoulders and sit in the right position.
창밖	outside the window	**창밖에 비가 오고 있었습니다.** It was raining outside the window.

풍경	scenery, landscape, view	산 정상에서 본 풍경이 진짜 아름다웠어요.
		The view from the top of the mountain was really beautiful.
어지럽다	to be dizzy	어지러우면 앉아서 잠깐 쉬세요.
		If you feel dizzy, sit down and rest for a while.
등	back	나 등 좀 긁어 줘.
		Please scratch my back.
건조하다	to be dry	겨울에는 날씨가 춥고 건조합니다.
		In winter, the weather is cold and dry.

Let's review!

Complete the story from Day 7 using the words you just learned.

지난주에 처음으로 비행기를 타 봤다.

_____ 정말 불편했다.

먼저 _____ _____ _____이 좁아서 다리를 ___ 수가 없었다.

그리고 내 자리에서는 _____ _____이 안 보였다.

답답하고 _____.

계속 앉아 있어서 ___이 아팠다.

비행기 안이 _____ 코도 아팠다.

앞으로는 비행기 타는 일이 기대되지 않을 것 같다.

Translation

Last week, I took a plane for the first time. I was **looking forward to** it, but it was really uncomfortable. First, the **space in front of and behind** the **seat** was tight, so I could not **stretch** my legs. And from my seat, I could not see the **scenery outside the window**. I felt stuffy and **dizzy**. I was seated the whole time, so my **back** hurt. It was **dry** inside the plane, so my nose also hurt. From now on, I do not think I will be looking forward to taking a plane.

Word Search - Find 7 words out of the vocabulary you just learned in this chapter.

안	기	얼	손	여	하	공
에	대	터	좌	석	지	간
매	하	가	새	사	라	지
펴	다	울	굴	풍	경	요
우	조	무	즘	활	생	막
앞	뒤	미	건	조	하	다
객	공	요	규	죄	해	텃

....

Fill in the blanks with Korean words that matches its English translation.

Word bank	
기대하다	창밖
좌석	풍경
앞뒤	어지럽다
공간	등
펴다	건조하다

01 space, room

_____

02 back

_____

03 outside the window

_____

04 to be dizzy

_____

05 seat

_____

Day 08

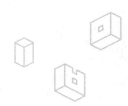

- 서로 ----------------------- ○
- 별명 ----------------------- ○
- 반말 ----------------------- ○
- 마음대로 ------------------ ○
- 반팔 ----------------------- ○
- 슬리퍼 -------------------- ○
- 자유롭다 ------------------ ○
- 굉장히 -------------------- ○
- 낯설다 -------------------- ○
- 익숙하다 ------------------ ○

Day 08   Let's warm up!

....

*Imagine the situation in the story below to
remember the ten Korean words in context.*

우리 회사 사람들은 **서로 별명**을 부르고 **반말**을 한다.

People in our company call **each other** by **nicknames** and use **casual speech**.

그래서 나이 차이를 신경 쓰지 않아도 된다.

So you do not have to care about age differences.

출근할 때 옷도 **마음대로** 입을 수 있다.

When you go to work, you can wear any style of clothes **as you please**.

여름에는 **반팔**, 반바지를 입고 **슬리퍼**를 신어도 된다.

In summer, you can wear **short sleeves**, shorts, and **flip-flops**.

처음에는 이런 **자유로운** 문화가 **굉장히 낯설었다**.

At first, this kind of **free** culture was **very** **unfamiliar** to me.

그런데 지금은 **익숙하고** 좋다.

But now, it is **familiar** to me and feels good.

Let's keep the ball rolling!

Word	Meaning	Example
서로	each other	학생들이 서로 도와서 이 로봇을 만들었어요. The students helped each other to build this robot.
별명	nickname	너 어릴 때 별명 있었어? Did you have a nickname when you were little?
반말	casual language, informal language	친한 친구들한테는 반말해도 돼요. You can use casual language with your close friends.
마음대로	as one pleases, at one's will	네 마음대로 해도 돼. You can do as you please.
반팔	short sleeves	더우면 반팔 셔츠로 갈아입어. If you are hot, change into a short-sleeved shirt.
슬리퍼	flip-flops, slippers	여기 슬리퍼 팔아요? Do you sell flip-flops here?

자유롭다

to be free

우리 학교는 다른 학교보다 규정이
자유로운 편이에요.

Our school's rules are freer than those of other
schools.

굉장히

very, extremely

죽이 굉장히 부드럽고 맛있네요.

The porridge is very smooth and delicious.

낯설다

to be unfamiliar,
to be strange

처음이어서 조금 낯설지만 괜찮아요.

This is my first time, so it's a little bit unfamiliar,
but I'm okay.

익숙하다

to be familiar,
to be used to

저한테 익숙한 일은 아니지만 해 볼게요.

It's not something I'm used to, but I'll try.

Let's review!

Complete the story from Day 8 using the words you just learned.

우리 회사 사람들은 _____ _____을 부르고 _____을 한다.

그래서 나이 차이를 신경 쓰지 않아도 된다.

출근할 때 옷도 _____ 입을 수 있다.

여름에는 _____, 반바지를 입고 _____를 신어도 된다.

처음에는 이런 _____ 문화가 _____ _____.

그런데 지금은 _____ 좋다.

Translation

People in our company call <u>each other</u> by <u>nicknames</u> and use <u>casual speech</u>. So you do not have to care about age differences. When you go to work, you can wear any style of clothes <u>as you please</u>. In summer, you can wear <u>short sleeves</u>, shorts, and <u>flip-flops</u>. At first, this kind of <u>free</u> culture was <u>very</u> <u>unfamiliar</u> to me. But now, it is <u>familiar</u> to me and feels good.

Crossword Puzzle

01 casual language, informal language

02 short sleeves

03 each other

04 as one pleases, at one's will

05 very, extremely

06 to be unfamiliar, to be strange

07 to be free

Fill in the blanks with Korean words that matches its English translation.

Word bank	
서로	슬리퍼
별명	자유롭다
반말	굉장히
마음대로	낯설다
반팔	익숙하다

01 flip-flops, slippers _____

02 to be familiar, to be used to _____

03 as one pleases, at one's will _____

04 each other _____

05 nickname _____

Day 09

Let's warm up!

Imagine the situation in the story below to
remember the ten Korean words in context.

나는 이상하게 중요한 일이 있을 때 **늦잠**을 잔다.
Strangely, I <u>oversleep</u> when I have something important to do.

학교 **대표**로 **발표** 대회에 나갔을 때도 늦잠을 잤다.
When I participated in the <u>presentation</u> contest as a <u>representative</u>
for my school, I overslept.

그래서 안 좋은 **평가**를 받았다.
So I got a bad <u>evaluation</u>.

회사 **면접** 때도 **지각했다**.
I <u>was late</u> for my <u>job interview</u> with my company, too.

늦잠이 내 **인생**을 **방해하고** 있는 것 같다.
I think oversleeping is <u>disrupting</u> my <u>life</u>.

이 나쁜 **버릇**을 버리고 빨리 문제를 **해결하고** 싶다.
I want to get rid of this bad <u>habit</u> and <u>solve</u> the problem quickly.

Let's keep the ball rolling!

Word	Meaning	Example
늦잠	oversleeping	나 오늘도 늦잠 잤어. I overslept again today.
대표	representative	그 그림은 한국 미술의 대표 작품입니다. The painting is a representative work of Korean art.
발표	presentation	발표를 하고 싶은 사람이 아무도 없어요? Is there no one who wants to make a presentation?
평가	evaluation, assessment	이번 시험에서 좋은 평가를 많이 받았어요. I got a lot of good evaluations on this test.
면접	job interview	면접 준비는 잘했어? Did you prepare well for the job interview?
지각하다	to be late, to be tardy	너 또 지각했니? Were you late again?

| 인생 | life | 인생은 짧고 예술은 길다는 말이 있어요. |
| | | There is a saying that life is short and art is long. |

| 방해하다 | to interrupt, to disturb, to disrupt | 나 공부할 거니까 방해하지 마. |
| | | I'm going to study, so don't disturb me. |

| 버릇 | habit | 저는 다리를 떠는 버릇이 있어요. |
| | | I have a habit of shaking my legs. |

| 해결하다 | to solve | 금방 해결할 수 있으니까 걱정할 필요 없어요. |
| | | I can solve it soon so you don't need to worry. |

Let's review!

Complete the story from Day 9 using the words you just learned.

나는 이상하게 중요한 일이 있을 때 _____을 잔다.

학교 _____로 _____ 대회에 나갔을 때도 늦잠을 잤다.

그래서 안 좋은 _____를 받았다.

회사 _____ 때도 _____.

늦잠이 내 _____을 _____ 있는 것 같다.

이 나쁜 _____을 버리고 빨리 문제를 _____ 싶다.

Translation

Strangely, I <u>oversleep</u> when I have something important to do. When I participated in the <u>presentation</u> contest as a <u>representative</u> for my school, I overslept. So I got a bad <u>evaluation</u>. I <u>was late</u> for my <u>job interview</u> with my company, too. I think oversleeping is <u>disrupting</u> my <u>life</u>. I want to get rid of this bad <u>habit</u> and <u>solve</u> the problem quickly.

Word Search - Find 7 words out of the vocabulary you just learned in this chapter.

면	접	다	생	대	민	각
료	완	해	발	표	부	생
쥐	니	소	봉	룻	인	첩
평	가	히	방	해	하	다
감	본	땡	경	결	평	오
접	인	생	하	하	표	보
어	험	규	람	다	늦	승

Fill in the blanks with Korean words that matches its English translation.

Word bank	
늦잠	지각하다
대표	인생
발표	방해하다
평가	버릇
면접	해결하다

01 habit

_____

02 representative

_____

03 oversleeping

_____

04 evaluation, assessment

_____

05 to be late, to be tardy

_____

Day 10

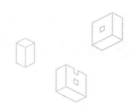

Day 10

Imagine the situation in the story below to
remember the ten Korean words in context.

오늘은 **조카**의 생일이다. 우리는 생일 파티를 준비했다.

Today is my <u>nephew</u>'s birthday. We prepared a birthday party.

서투르지만 음식도 **직접** 만들었다.

I <u>am not good</u> at it, but I also made the food <u>myself</u>.

그리고 선물로 **장난감**이랑 **인형**도 준비했다.

And I prepared a <u>toy</u> and a <u>doll</u> as gifts.

풍선으로 집도 **멋지게 꾸몄다**.

I also <u>decorated</u> the house <u>nicely</u> with <u>balloons</u>.

생일 파티 준비 때문에 **정신없는** 하루였다.

Because of all the birthday party preparations, it was a <u>hectic</u> day.

그래도 조카가 좋아할 것을 **상상하니까** 기분이 좋다.

Still, I feel happy <u>imagining</u> how my nephew will like it.

Let's keep the ball rolling!

Word	Meaning	Example
조카	nephew, niece	내년에 조카들이랑 제주도로 여행 갈 거예요. Next year I'll go on a trip to Jeju Island with my nephews and nieces.
서투르다	to be unskilled, to be not good	제가 영어에 좀 서툴러요. I'm not very good at English.
직접	for oneself, in person	내가 그 사람한테 직접 말할게. I'll speak to her myself.
장난감	toy, plaything	이제 장난감 그만 가지고 놀고 밥 먹자. Let's stop playing with toys now and have a meal.
인형	doll	제 동생은 항상 인형을 안고 자요. My sister always sleeps while hugging a doll.
풍선	balloon	풍선이 갑자기 터져서 깜짝 놀랐어. The balloon burst suddenly, so I was surprised.

멋지다	to be nice, to be wonderful	넌 정말 멋진 사람이야.
		You're such a wonderful person.

꾸미다	to decorate, to make up	이쪽 벽을 꽃으로 꾸미면 예쁠 것 같아요.
		I think it'd be pretty to decorate this wall with flowers.

정신없다	to be hectic, to be swamped, to be so busy	너무 정신없어서 네 전화 못 봤어.
		I was so busy so I couldn't see your call.

상상하다	to imagine	모두가 행복한 세상을 상상해 보세요.
		Imagine a world where everyone is happy.

Let's review!

Complete the story from Day 10 using the words you just learned.

오늘은 _____의 생일이다. 우리는 생일 파티를 준비했다.

_____ 음식도 _____ 만들었다.

그리고 선물로 _____이랑 _____도 준비했다.

_____으로 집도 _____ _____.

생일 파티 준비 때문에 _____ 하루였다.

그래도 조카가 좋아할 것을 _____ 기분이 좋다.

Translation

Today is my <u>nephew</u>'s birthday. We prepared a birthday party.
I <u>am not good</u> at it, but I also made the food <u>myself</u>. And I prepared
a <u>toy</u> and a <u>doll</u> as gifts. I also <u>decorated</u> the house <u>nicely</u> with
<u>balloons</u>. Because of all the birthday party preparations, it was a
<u>hectic</u> day. Still, I feel happy <u>imagining</u> how my nephew will like it.

Crossword Puzzle

		01		02		
			03		04	
05						
06				07		

01   to imagine

02   to decorate, to make up

03   to be hectic, to be swamped, to be so busy

04   nephew, niece

05   to be nice, to be wonderful

06   toy, plaything

07   for oneself, in person

Fill in the blanks with Korean words that matches its English translation.

Word bank	
조카	풍선
서투르다	멋지다
직접	꾸미다
장난감	정신없다
인형	상상하다

01   doll   _____

02   to decorate, to make up   _____

03   to be unskilled, to be not good   _____

04   balloon   _____

05   for oneself, in person   _____

01 How do you say "garlic" in Korean?

    a. 김치　　　　**b.** 마늘　　　　**c.** 차이　　　　**d.** 소금

02 Write the character that can fit in all of the blanks. _____

____정	____행	____기
= schedule	= group	= diary

03 Choose a term which is <u>not</u> related to emotions.

    a. 정신없다　　**b.** 아쉽다　　　**c.** 따라오다　　**d.** 감동하다

04 What is the antonym of 찬성하다? _____

05 Which of the following does <u>not</u> become a verb if you attach -하다?

    a. 좌석　　　　**b.** 작성　　　　**c.** 상상　　　　**d.** 노력

06 Choose an item you <u>cannot</u> buy as a gift.

    a. 인형   **b.** 장난감   **c.** 등   **d.** 슬리퍼

07 How do you say "nickname" in Korean?

    a. 역할   **b.** 인생   **c.** 인형   **d.** 별명

08 Write the character that can fit in all of the blanks. _____

제대____ = properly	마음대____ = as one pleases	서____ each other

09 What is the Korean word for the item in the picture? _____

10 Choose a term which is <u>not</u> related to family.

    a. 부모   **b.** 관객   **c.** 조카   **d.** 가정

11 저희 가족은 토요일마다 _____을/를 해요.

= My family eats out every Saturday.

12 _____이/가 오면 같이 주문할게요.

= I'll place an order together when my group arrives.

13 나 다음 주에 _____ 그 전에 만나자.

= I'm leaving the country next week, so let's meet before then.

14 고기를 다 _____ 다음에 양파를 넣습니다.

= After frying the meat, add the onion.

15 _____ 회사 앞에 택시가 있었어요.

= At the right time, there was a taxi in front of the company office.

16 다른 _____ 있으면 알려 주세요.

= Please let me know if you have any other opinions.

17 나는 _____이/가 있어서 오늘 모임에 못 갈 것 같아.

= I have a previous engagement, so I don't think I can go to the meeting today.

18 당신이 _____ 않기를 바라요.

= I hope you don't feel lonely.

19 _____ 앉아서 잠깐 쉬세요.

= If you feel dizzy, sit down and rest for a while.

20 죽이 _____ 부드럽고 맛있네요.

= The porridge is very smooth and delicious.

QUIZ
DAY 01-10

Day 11

성격 -------------------- ⬡

활발하다 ------------------ ⬡

부럽다 -------------------- ⬡

부족하다 ------------------ ⬡

겸손하다 ------------------ ⬡

장점 -------------------- ⬡

물론 -------------------- ⬡

단점 -------------------- ⬡

거절 -------------------- ⬡

들어주다 ------------------ ⬡

Day 11

Let's warm up!

Imagine the situation in the story below to
remember the ten Korean words in context.

내 친구는 공부를 잘하고 **성격**이 **활발하다**.
My friend is good at studying and has an <u>outgoing</u> <u>personality</u>.

정말 **부럽다**.
I am really <u>jealous</u>.

부족한 것이 없는 이 친구는 **겸손하기**까지 하다.
This friend, who <u>lacks</u> nothing, is even <u>humble</u>.

정말 **장점**이 많은 친구다.
My friend has a lot of <u>strengths</u>.

물론 이 친구에게도 **단점**은 있다.
<u>Of course</u>, this friend also has <u>weaknesses</u>.

이 친구는 **거절**을 잘 못한다.
This friend is not good at <u>refusing</u>.

그래서 다른 사람의 부탁을 다 **들어준다**.
So she <u>grants</u> all the requests of other people.

Let's keep the ball rolling!

Word	Meaning	Example
성격	character, personality	저랑 친구는 성격이 너무 달라요. My friend and I have very different personalities.
활발하다	to be active, to be outgoing	저는 성격이 활발한 사람이 좋아요. I like people who have an outgoing personality.
부럽다	to be envious, to be jealous	동생이 있는 사람이 부러워요. I'm jealous of people who have a younger sibling.
부족하다	to be insufficient, to lack	아직 부족한 게 많습니다. I still lack a lot.
겸손하다	to be humble, to be modest	너무 겸손할 필요는 없어요. You don't have to be too humble.
장점	advantage, strength, strong point	저의 장점은 꼼꼼하다는 것입니다. My strength is that I'm meticulous.

물론 of course 물론 현우 씨가 제일 늦게 왔어요.
Of course Hyunwoo was the last person to come.

단점 weakness, flaw 단점이 없는 사람은 없습니다.
There's no one who is flawless.

거절 refusal, rejection 어떻게 하면 거절을 잘할 수 있을까?
How can I be good at refusing?

들어주다 to grant 제 소원 좀 들어주세요.
Please grant me a wish.

Let's review!

Complete the story from Day 11 using the words you just learned.

내 친구는 공부를 잘하고 _____이 _____.

정말 _____.

_____ 것이 없는 이 친구는 _____까지 하다.

정말 _____이 많은 친구다.

_____이 친구에게도 _____은 있다.

이 친구는 _____을 잘 못한다.

그래서 다른 사람의 부탁을 다 _____.

Translation

My friend is good at studying and has an <u>outgoing personality</u>.
I am really <u>jealous</u>. This friend, who <u>lacks</u> nothing, is even <u>humble</u>.
My friend has a lot of <u>strengths</u>. <u>Of course</u>, this friend also has
<u>weaknesses</u>. This friend is not good at <u>refusing</u>. So she <u>grants</u> all
the requests of other people.

Word Search - Find 7 words out of the vocabulary you just learned in this chapter.

잠	세	물	론	잔	소	부
성	혜	절	라	하	린	럽
격	장	럽	단	점	대	다
지	물	활	둥	격	샤	구
요	현	발	겨	론	거	소
겸	손	하	다	쇼	절	데
부	점	다	지	으	머	라

Fill in the blanks with Korean words that matches its English translation.

Word bank	
성격	장점
활발하다	물론
부럽다	단점
부족하다	거절
겸손하다	들어주다

01 to be insufficient, to lack

_____

02 refusal, rejection

_____

03 advantage, strength, strong point

_____

04 of course

_____

05 to grant

_____

Day 12

Day 12

Let's warm up!

Imagine the situation in the story below to
remember the ten Korean words in context.

요즘 내 몸에 몇 가지 **변화**가 생겼다.
Recently, there have been a few **changes** in my body.

계속 **졸리고 하품**을 많이 한다.
I am always feeling **sleepy**, and I **yawn** a lot.

피부가 건조하고 **여드름**이 많이 생겼다.
My **skin** is dry and I got a lot of **pimples**.

그리고 **머리카락**도 **점점** 많이 **빠지는** 것 같다.
And my **hair** seems to be **falling out** **more and more**.

병원에 가니까 의사가 **푹** 쉬라고 했다.
I went to the hospital and the doctor told me to rest **well**.

그동안 **피로**가 쌓였었나 보다.
I guess my **fatigue** has been piling up.

Let's keep the ball rolling!

Word	Meaning	Example
변화	change	변화에 잘 적응하는 사람이 부러워요. I'm jealous of people who adapt well to change.
졸리다	to be[feel] sleepy	졸리면 잠깐 나갔다가 오세요. If you're sleepy, go out for a while and come back.
하품	yawn	어제 잠을 잘 못 자서 하품이 계속 나와요. I didn't sleep well yesterday, so I keep yawning.
피부	skin	저는 일주일에 한 번 피부 관리를 받아요. I get skin treatment once a week.
여드름	pimple, acne	엄청 큰 여드름이 났어요. I got a really big pimple.
머리카락	hair	머리카락에 껌이 붙었어요. Some gum was stuck to my hair.

점점	gradually	혼자 사는 사람들이 점점 많아지고 있습니다.
		There are more and more people living alone.
빠지다	to fall out, to lose	아이스크림을 먹고 있는데, 이가 빠졌어요.
		I was eating ice cream when my tooth fell out.
푹	well	잠을 푹 자서 기분이 너무 좋아요.
		I feel very good because I slept well.
피로	fatigue, tiredness	따뜻한 물로 목욕을 하니까 피로가 풀리는 것 같아요.
		Taking a hot bath seems to relieve my fatigue.

Let's review!

....

Complete the story from Day 12 using the words you just learned.

요즘 내 몸에 몇 가지 _____가 생겼다.

계속 _____ _____을 많이 한다.

_____가 건조하고 _____이 많이 생겼다.

그리고 _____도 _____ 많이 _____ 것 같다.

병원에 가니까 의사가 ___ 쉬라고 했다.

그동안 _____가 쌓였었나 보다.

....

Translation

Recently, there have been a few **changes** in my body. I am always feeling **sleepy**, and I **yawn** a lot. My **skin** is dry and I got a lot of **pimples**. And my **hair** seems to be **falling out** **more and more**. I went to the hospital and the doctor told me to rest **well**. I guess my **fatigue** has been piling up.

Crossword Puzzle

					01		
	02						
03					04		
			05				
	06					07	

01 skin

02 hair

03 yawn

04 pimple, acne

05 to fall out, to lose

06 to be[feel] sleepy

07 fatigue, tiredness

Fill in the blanks with Korean words that matches its English translation.

Word bank	
변화	머리카락
졸리다	점점
하품	빠지다
피부	푹
여드름	피로

01 well _____

02 gradually _____

03 change _____

04 yawn _____

05 to be[feel] sleepy _____

Day 13

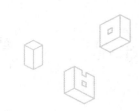

Day 13

Imagine the situation in the story below to
remember the ten Korean words in context.

집 앞 정원에 꽃을 **심었다**.

I __planted__ flowers in the garden in front of my house.

베란다에 있는 **화분**에도 꽃을 심었다.

I also planted flowers in the __flower pots__ that are on the __balcony__.

잘 **가꾸어** 주니까 꽃이 예쁘게 **피었다**.

I __grew__ the flowers well, so the flowers __bloomed__ beautifully.

그런데 갑자기 **장마**가 시작돼서 비가 **오랫동안** 내렸다.

But the __rainy season__ suddenly started, and it rained __for a long time__.

장마 때문에 **야외**에 심은 꽃은 다 죽었다.

Because of the rainy season, all the flowers that I planted __outside__
died.

실내에 심은 꽃만 살았다.

Only the flowers that I planted __inside__ survived.

이런 일을 **막기** 위해서 앞으로는 실내에만 꽃을 심을 것이다.

To __prevent__ this from happening, I will only plant flowers inside
from now on.

Let's keep the ball rolling!

Word	Meaning	Example
심다	to plant	작년에 제가 심은 나무예요. This is a tree that I planted last year.
베란다	indoor balcony with windows (commonly seen in Korean)	냄새 나니까 베란다 창문 좀 열어 주세요. It smells bad, so please open the balcony windows.
화분	flower pot	아이가 실수로 화분을 깼어요. The child broke a flower pot by mistake.
가꾸다	to grow	식물을 가꾸는 게 취미예요. Growing plants is my hobby.
피다	to bloom	꽃이 너무 예쁘게 폈네요. The flowers bloomed so beautifully!
장마	rainy season, monsoon	다음 주부터 장마가 시작된다고 합니다. The rainy season is said to start next week.

오랫동안	for a long time	저 진짜 오랫동안 기다렸어요. I waited for a really long time.
야외	outside	날씨가 좋으면 야외에서 식사할 거예요. If the weather is good, we'll eat outside.
실내	inside	비가 오면 실내에서 놀면 돼요. If it rains, we can play inside.
막다	to prevent, to stop	싸움을 막으려고 노력했는데 잘 안 됐어요. I tried to prevent the fight, but it didn't work.

Let's review!

Complete the story from Day 13 using the words you just learned.

집 앞 정원에 꽃을 _____.

_____에 있는 _____에도 꽃을 심었다.

잘 _____ 주니까 꽃이 예쁘게 _____.

그런데 갑자기 _____가 시작돼서 비가 _____ 내렸다.

장마 때문에 _____에 심은 꽃은 다 죽었다.

_____에 심은 꽃만 살았다.

이런 일을 _____ 위해서 앞으로는 실내에만 꽃을 심을 것이다.

Translation

I <u>planted</u> flowers in the garden in front of my house. I also planted flowers in the <u>flower pots</u> that are on the <u>balcony</u>. I <u>grew</u> the flowers well, so the flowers <u>bloomed</u> beautifully. But the <u>rainy season</u> suddenly started, and it rained <u>for a long time</u>. Because of the rainy season, all the flowers that I planted <u>outside</u> died. Only the flowers that I planted <u>inside</u> survived. To <u>prevent</u> this from happening, I will only plant flowers inside from now on.

Word Search - Find 7 words out of the vocabulary you just learned in this chapter.

가	더	심	다	은	야	라
지	경	소	추	여	외	막
화	분	다	둥	피	헌	안
중	람	진	섬	다	배	네
랫	장	마	화	경	란	실
바	머	욱	다	예	다	내
차	오	랫	동	안	희	마

Fill in the blanks with Korean words that matches its English translation.

Word bank	
심다	장마
베란다	오랫동안
화분	야외
가꾸다	실내
피다	막다

01 to grow

_____

02 to prevent, to stop

_____

03 flower pot

_____

04 for a long time

_____

05 indoor balcony with windows

_____

Day 14

종일	
꽤	
보고서	
제출하다	
전날	
야근하다	
겨우	
마치다	
회식	
기억나다	

Day 14

Let's warm up!

Imagine the situation in the story below to
remember the ten Korean words in context.

오늘 하루 종일 꽤 바빴다.

I have been <u>pretty</u> busy <u>all day</u> today.

퇴근 전까지 보고서를 제출해야 했기 때문이다.

It was because I had to <u>submit</u> my <u>report</u> before leaving the office.

전날 야근해서 퇴근 전에 겨우 일을 마칠 수
있었다.

I <u>worked overtime the day before</u>, so I was just <u>barely</u> able to
<u>finish</u> my work before leaving the office.

일을 마친 뒤, 빨리 집에 가려고 했다.

After finishing work, I was planning to go home quickly.

그런데 갑자기 오늘 회식이 있는 게 기억났다.

But then suddenly I <u>remembered</u> that there was a <u>company</u>
<u>gathering</u> today.

회식까지 다녀오니까 정말 피곤했다.

After the company gathering, I felt really tired.

Let's keep the ball rolling!

Word	Meaning	Example
종일	all day (long), the whole day	하루 종일 이것밖에 못 했어요? You only did this much all day long?
꽤	quite, pretty	그 호텔 꽤 괜찮았어. The hotel was pretty good.
보고서	report	내일 회의 전까지 보고서를 써야 돼요. Before tomorrow's meeting, I have to write a report.
제출하다	to submit	보고서 제출하기 전에 적어도 세 번은 읽어 보세요. Before submitting the report, please read it at least three times.
전날	the day before	크리스마스 전날에는 항상 가족들과 함께 저녁 식사를 해요. The day before Christmas, I always have dinner with my family.
야근하다	to work overtime	요즘 매일 야근해서 피곤해요. I've been working overtime every day lately, so I'm tired.

| **겨우** | barely | 비행기가 출발하기 전에 겨우 탔어요. |
| | | I barely got on the airplane before it took off. |

| **마치다** | to end, to finish | 오늘 오전까지 다 마쳐야 돼요. |
| | | I have to finish everything by this morning. |

| **회식** | company gathering | 저희 회사는 점심시간에 회식을 해요. |
| | | Our company has a company gathering at lunchtime. |

| **기억나다** | to remember | 저는 어렸을 때 일이 다 기억나요. |
| | | I remember everything that happened when I was young. |

Let's review!

Complete the story from Day 14 using the words you just learned.

오늘 하루 _____ ___ 바빴다.

퇴근 전까지 _____를 _____ 했기 때문이다.

_____ _____ 퇴근 전에 _____ 일을 _____ 수 있었다.

일을 마친 뒤, 빨리 집에 가려고 했다.

그런데 갑자기 오늘 _____이 있는 게 _____.

회식까지 다녀오니까 정말 피곤했다.

....

Translation

I have been <u>pretty</u> busy <u>all day</u> today. It was because I had to <u>submit</u> my <u>report</u> before leaving the office. I <u>worked overtime</u> <u>the day</u> <u>before</u>, so I was just <u>barely</u> able to <u>finish</u> my work before leaving the office. After finishing work, I was planning to go home quickly. But then suddenly I <u>remembered</u> that there was a <u>company gathering</u> today. After the company gathering, I felt really tired.

Crossword Puzzle

01				02			
		03					
	04			05			
			06				
07							

01 the day before

02 to end, to finish

03 company gathering

04 report

05 barely

06 to remember

07 all day (long), the whole day

Fill in the blanks with Korean words that matches its English translation.

Word bank	
종일	야근하다
꽤	겨우
보고서	마치다
제출하다	회식
전날	기억나다

01 to remember _____

02 quite, pretty _____

03 barely _____

04 to work overtime _____

05 to submit _____

Day 15

Day 15

Let's warm up!

....

Imagine the situation in the story below to
remember the ten Korean words in context.

오늘 아침에 책상 위에 우유를 **올려놓았는데** 실수로 **쏟았다**.

This morning, I <u>put</u> my milk <u>on</u> the desk and I <u>spilled</u> it by mistake.

쏟은 우유를 닦다가 **걸레**를 **밟고** 넘어졌다.

While wiping the spilled milk, I <u>stepped on</u> a <u>rag</u> and fell down.

엉덩이에 우유가 **묻었다**.

My <u>butt</u> was <u>stained with</u> milk.

그리고 일어나다가 **탁자** 다리를 **찼다**.

And as I was getting up, I <u>kicked</u> the leg of the <u>table</u>.

발가락 **뼈**가 **부러졌다**.

My toe <u>bone was broken</u>.

정말 힘든 하루였다.

It was a really tough day.

Let's keep the ball rolling!

Word	Meaning	Example
올려놓다	to put (on), to be on	그냥 의자 위에 올려놔 주세요. Just put it on the chair.
쏟다	to spill	친구 노트북에 커피를 쏟았어요. I spilled coffee on my friend's laptop.
걸레	rag	걸레로 부엌 바닥 좀 닦아 주세요. Please wipe the kitchen floor with a rag.
밟다	to step on	아, 너 지금 내 발 밟고 있어! Ouch, you're stepping on my foot!
엉덩이	butt, bottom	감기에 걸려서 엉덩이에 주사를 맞았어요. I caught a cold, so I got an injection in my butt.
묻다	to be stained with, to be[get] on something	얼굴에 뭐가 묻었어요. You've got something on your face.

탁자	table	탁자가 너무 오래돼서 새로 사야 돼요. The table is too old, so I have to buy a new one.
차다	to kick	영화관에서 앞 좌석을 발로 차지 마세요. Don't kick the seat in front of you in the movie theater.
뼈	bone	나이가 들수록 뼈 건강에 신경을 더 써야 해요. The older you get, the more attention you should pay to your bone health.
부러지다	to be[get] broken	팔이 부러진 것 같아요. I think my arm is broken.

Let's review!

Complete the story from Day 15 using the words you just learned.

오늘 아침에 책상 위에 우유를 ＿＿＿＿＿＿＿ 실수로 ＿＿＿＿.

쏟은 우유를 닦다가 ＿＿＿를 ＿＿＿ 넘어졌다.

＿＿＿＿＿에 우유가 ＿＿＿＿.

그리고 일어나다가 ＿＿＿ 다리를 ＿＿＿.

발가락 ＿＿＿가 ＿＿＿＿＿＿.

정말 힘든 하루였다.

Translation

This morning, I <u>put</u> my milk <u>on</u> the desk and I <u>spilled</u> it by mistake. While wiping the spilled milk, I <u>stepped on</u> a <u>rag</u> and fell down. My <u>butt</u> was <u>stained with</u> milk. And as I was getting up, I <u>kicked</u> the leg of the <u>table</u>. My toe <u>bone</u> <u>was broken</u>. It was a really tough day.

Word Search - Find 7 words out of the vocabulary you just learned in this chapter.

주	나	법	쏟	다	묻	등
걸	턱	자	솔	후	밟	늘
레	도	부	러	지	다	이
미	솔	희	치	전	단	출
웅	탁	자	대	나	따	묻
동	소	레	고	강	증	다
이	고	차	다	비	부	저

Fill in the blanks with Korean words that matches its English translation.

Word bank	
올려놓다	묻다
쏟다	탁자
걸레	차다
밟다	뼈
엉덩이	부러지다

01 butt, bottom

_____

02 to be[get] broken

_____

03 bone

_____

04 to step on

_____

05 to spill

_____

Day 16

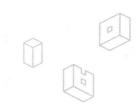

⬡	손자 -----------------	⬡
⬡	돌보다 ----------------	⬡
⬡	누르다 ----------------	⬡
⬡	닮다 ------------------	⬡
⬡	주방 ------------------	⬡
⬡	미술 ------------------	⬡
⬡	학원 ------------------	⬡
⬡	악기 ------------------	⬡
⬡	연주하다 --------------	⬡
⬡	도움 ------------------	⬡

Day 16

Let's warm up!

Imagine the situation in the story below to
remember the ten Korean words in context.

오랜만에 **손자**를 **돌봐** 주러 딸 집에 갔다.

For the first time in a while, I went to my daughter's house to
<u>look after</u> my <u>grandson</u>.

딸 집 앞에 도착해서 벨을 **눌렀다**.

I arrived in front of my daughter's house and <u>pressed</u> the doorbell.

나를 **닮은** 손자가 문을 열어 줬다.

My grandson, who <u>looks like</u> me, opened the door.

딸은 **주방**에서 요리를 하고 있었다.

My daughter was cooking in the <u>kitchen</u>.

나는 손자의 **미술 학원** 숙제를 도와줬다.

I helped with my grandson's <u>art</u> <u>academy</u> homework.

악기 연주하는 것도 도와줬다.

I also helped him with <u>playing</u> his <u>musical instrument</u>.

딸에게 **도움**을 준 것 같아서 기쁜 하루였다.

It was a good day because I felt like I <u>helped</u> my daughter.

Let's keep the ball rolling!

Word	Meaning	Example
손자	grandson	우리 손자가 다음 달에 결혼을 해요. My grandson is going to get married next month.
돌보다	to look after	친구가 고양이를 돌봐 줄 거예요. My friend will look after my cat.
누르다	to press, to push	엘리베이터 버튼을 너무 여러 번 누르지 마세요. Don't push the elevator buttons too many times.
닮다	to resemble, to look like	저는 엄마랑 아빠 둘 다 안 닮았어요. I neither look like my mom nor my dad.
주방	kitchen	주방이 좁아서 요리하기가 불편해요. The kitchen is small, so it's inconvenient to cook in.
미술	art	저는 미술 시간을 제일 좋아해요. I like art class the most.

학원	private academy, after-school program (commonly seen in Korea)	오늘 저녁에 피아노 학원 가요? Are you going to the piano school tonight?
악기	musical instrument	어떤 악기를 배우고 싶어요? What kind of musical instrument do you want to learn?
연주하다	to perform, to play	이번 주 토요일에 학교에서 피아노를 연주해요. I'm going to play the piano at school this Saturday.
도움	help	도움이 필요할 때 연락 주세요. Contact me when you need help.

Let's review!

Complete the story from Day 16 using the words you just learned.

오랜만에 _____를 _____ 주러 딸 집에 갔다.

딸 집 앞에 도착해서 벨을 _____.

나를 _____ 손자가 문을 열어 줬다.

딸은 _____에서 요리를 하고 있었다.

나는 손자의 _____ _____ 숙제를 도와줬다.

_____ _____ 것도 도와줬다.

딸에게 _____을 준 것 같아서 기쁜 하루였다.

Translation

For the first time in a while, I went to my daughter's house to <u>look after</u> my <u>grandson</u>. I arrived in front of my daughter's house and <u>pressed</u> the doorbell. My grandson, who <u>looks like</u> me, opened the door. My daughter was cooking in the <u>kitchen</u>. I helped with my grandson's <u>art academy</u> homework. I also helped him with <u>playing</u> his <u>musical instrument</u>. It was a good day because I felt like I <u>helped</u> my daughter.

Crossword Puzzle

		01				02
03				04		
05						
					06	
	07					

01 to resemble, to look like

02 private academy, after-school program (commonly seen in Korea)

03 to look after

04 to press, to push

05 kitchen

06 art

07 help

....

Fill in the blanks with Korean words that matches its English translation.

Word bank	
손자	미술
돌보다	학원
누르다	악기
닮다	연주하다
주방	도움

01 kitchen   _____

02 to perform, to play   _____

03 to press, to push   _____

04 grandson   _____

05 musical instrument   _____

Day 17

Day 17

Let's warm up!

....

Imagine the situation in the story below to remember the ten Korean words in context.

천둥, 번개 때문에 **밤새** 잠을 못 잤다.

Because of the **thunder** and **lightning**, I could not sleep at all **all night long**.

그래서 늦잠을 잤다.

Therefore, I overslept.

모임에 늦을 것 같아서 택시를 탔다.

I thought I would be late for the meeting, so I took a taxi.

이 모임은 늦으면 벌금을 내야 한다.

If I am late for this meeting, I will have to pay a **fine**.

나는 차에서 내리자마자 뛰었다.

As soon as I got out of the car, I ran.

길이 미끄러워서 넘어졌다.

The street was **slippery**, so I fell down.

스타킹에 구멍이 났다.

I got a **hole** in my **stockings**.

당장 새 스타킹을 구할 수 없어서 당황했다.

I could not **get** new stockings **right away**, so I **did not know what to do**.

Let's keep the ball rolling!

Word	Meaning	Example
천둥	thunder	천둥 소리가 너무 커서 무서워요. The sound of thunder is too loud, so I get scared.
번개	lightning	방금 번개 치는 거 봤어? Did you just see the lightning?
밤새	all night long, through the night	내일 시험이 있어서 밤새 공부했어요. I have an exam tomorrow, so I studied all night long.
벌금	fine, penalty	1분이라도 늦으면 벌금을 내야 돼요. If you're even a minute late, you have to pay a fine.
미끄럽다	to be slippery	눈이 와서 길이 미끄러워요. It's snowing, so the street is slippery.
스타킹	(a pair of) stockings	편의점에서 스타킹을 살 수 있어요. We can buy stockings at convenience stores.

| 구멍 | hole | 바지에 구멍이 나서 갈아입었어요. |
| | | My pants got a hole, so I changed them. |

| 당장 | right away, immediately | 지금 당장 저한테 와 줄 수 있어요? |
| | | Can you come to me right now? |

| 구하다 | to obtain, to get | 이 자료 어디서 구했어요? |
| | | Where did you get this data? |

| 당황하다 | to be bewildered, to not know what to do | 너무 당황해서 아무 말도 못 했어요. |
| | | I was so bewildered, so I couldn't say anything. |

Let's review!

Complete the story from Day 17 using the words you just learned.

_____, _____ 때문에 _____ 잠을 못 잤다.

그래서 늦잠을 잤다.

모임에 늦을 것 같아서 택시를 탔다.

이 모임은 늦으면 _____을 내야 한다.

나는 차에서 내리자마자 뛰었다.

길이 _____ 넘어졌다.

_____에 _____이 났다.

_____ 새 스타킹을 _____ 수 없어서 _____.

Translation

Because of the **thunder** and **lightning**, I could not sleep at all **all night long**. Therefore, I overslept. I thought I would be late for the meeting, so I took a taxi. If I am late for this meeting, I will have to pay a **fine**. As soon as I got out of the car, I ran. The street was **slippery**, so I fell down. I got a **hole** in my **stockings**. I could not **get** new stockings **right away**, so I **did not know what to do**.

Word Search – Find 7 words out of the vocabulary you just learned in this chapter.

소	벌	금	다	저	허	구
당	희	초	나	됴	다	하
밤	개	후	천	둥	현	다
새	윤	루	동	소	두	지
황	지	다	고	당	장	추
구	망	연	항	숭	다	윤
멍	혜	경	당	황	하	다

Fill in the blanks with Korean words that matches its English translation.

Word bank	
천둥	스타킹
번개	구멍
밤새	당장
벌금	구하다
미끄럽다	당황하다

01 lightning _____

02 (a pair of) stockings _____

03 to obtain, to get _____

04 hole _____

05 to be slippery _____

Day 18

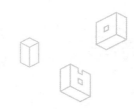

Day 18

Let's warm up!

....

Imagine the situation in the story below to remember the ten Korean words in context.

서랍을 **정리하다가** 부모님 옛날 사진을 **우연히** 봤다.

While <u>organizing</u> the <u>drawers</u>, I saw an old photo of my parents <u>by chance</u>.

아빠가 카메라로 엄마를 **촬영하고** 있는 사진이었다.

It was a picture of my dad <u>filming</u> my mom with a camera.

엄마는 **연기**를 하고 있는 것 같았다.

It looked like my mom was <u>acting</u>.

엄마한테 물어보니까 학교 **축제** 때 사진이라고 했다.

I asked my mom, and she said it was a picture from her school <u>festival</u>.

그때 아빠는 영화 **동아리 회장**이었고, 엄마는 **신입생**이었다.

At that time, my dad was the <u>president</u> of the film <u>club</u>, and my mom was a <u>freshman</u>.

부모님이 **젊으셨을** 때 모습을 보니까 신기했다.

It was amazing to see what my parents looked like when they were <u>young</u>.

Let's keep the ball rolling!

Word	Meaning	Example
서랍	drawer	아, 서류는 첫 번째 서랍에 넣어 놓았어요. Ah, I put the document in the first drawer.
정리하다	to organize	책상 위에 있는 물건 좀 정리하세요. Please organize the stuff on your desk.
우연히	by chance, by accident	길을 걷다가 우연히 친구를 만났어요. While I was walking down the street, I saw my friend by chance.
촬영하다	to film, to shoot	드라마 촬영하고 있는 사람들을 봤어요. I saw people filming a TV show.
연기	acting	다음 달부터 연기 수업을 들을 거예요. Starting from next month, I'm going to take an acting class.
축제	festival	유명한 연예인이 이번 축제에 온다고 들었어요. I heard that a famous celebrity is coming to this festival.

동아리	club (for student's activities)	어떤 동아리에 들어갈 거야? Which club will you join?
회장	president	제가 이 모임 회장이에요. I'm the president of this club.
신입생	freshman	신입생들이 이번에 많이 들어왔어요. A lot of freshmen joined this time.
젊다	to be young	아직 젊으니까 너무 걱정하지 말아요. You're still young, so don't worry too much.

Let's review!

Complete the story from Day 18 using the words you just learned.

_____을 _____ 부모님 옛날 사진을 _____ 봤다.

아빠가 카메라로 엄마를 _____ 있는 사진이었다.

엄마는 _____를 하고 있는 것 같았다.

엄마한테 물어보니까 학교 _____ 때 사진이라고 했다.

그때 아빠는 영화 _____ _____이었고, 엄마는 _____이
었다.

부모님이 _____ 때 모습을 보니까 신기했다.

Translation

While **organizing** the **drawers**, I saw an old photo of my parents **by chance**. It was a picture of my dad **filming** my mom with a camera. It looked like my mom was **acting**. I asked my mom, and she said it was a picture from her school **festival**. At that time, my dad was the **president** of the film **club**, and my mom was a **freshman**. It was amazing to see what my parents looked like when they were **young**.

Crossword Puzzle

01 drawer

02 club (for student's activities)

03 festival

04 to be young

05 by chance, by accident

06 acting

07 president

Fill in the blanks with Korean words that matches its English translation.

Word bank	
서랍	축제
정리하다	동아리
우연히	회장
촬영하다	신입생
연기	젊다

01 to organize _____

02 freshman _____

03 festival _____

04 to film, to shoot _____

05 drawer _____

Day 19

- **치과** ------------------- ◯
- **깔끔하다** --------------- ◯
- **썩다** ------------------- ◯
- **창피하다** --------------- ◯
- **습관** ------------------- ◯
- **결심하다** --------------- ◯
- **미루다** ----------------- ◯
- **약간** ------------------- ◯
- **노랗다** ----------------- ◯
- **훨씬** ------------------- ◯

Day 19

Let's warm up!

Imagine the situation in the story below to
remember the ten Korean words in context.

이가 아파서 **치과**에 갔다.

I had a toothache, so I went to the <u>dentist's office</u>.

새로 생긴 치과라서 **깔끔했다**.

It was a new dentist's office, so it was <u>neat and tidy</u>.

의사 선생님이 내 이가 **썩었다고** 했다.

The dentist said I had some <u>decayed</u> teeth.

조금 **창피했다**.

I was a little <u>embarrassed</u>.

이를 잘 닦는 **습관**을 기를 것이라고 **결심했다**.

I <u>made up my mind</u> that I would make a <u>habit</u> of brushing my teeth well.

이제는 이 닦는 것을 **미루지** 않을 것이다.

I will not <u>put off</u> brushing my teeth anymore.

또 선생님은 내 이가 **약간 노랗다고** 했다.

The dentist also said that my teeth are <u>a little</u> <u>yellow</u>.

그리고 이를 하얗게 만들어 줬다.

And she made my teeth white.

훨씬 보기 좋아져서 기분이 좋다.

They look <u>much</u> better, so I feel good.

Let's keep the ball rolling!

Word	Meaning	Example
치과	dentist's office, dental clinic	치과 가는 게 제일 무서워요. Going to the dentist's office is the scariest thing.
깔끔하다	to be clean, to be neat and tidy	방이 너무 깔끔해서 놀랐어요. I was surprised because your room was so neat and tidy.
썩다	to decay	이가 썩어서 치료를 받았어요. My teeth were decayed, so I got treatment.
창피하다	to be embarrassed, to be ashamed	창피해할 필요 없어. You don't need to be embarrassed.
습관	habit	아침밥을 먹는 습관이 생겼어요. I got into the habit of eating breakfast.
결심하다	to make up one's mind, to decide	언제 결혼을 결심했어요? When did you decide to get married?

| **미루다** | to put off | 할 일을 미루지 마세요. |
| | | Don't put off things to do. |

| **약간** | a little, a bit | 약간 배고픈 것 같아요. |
| | | I think I'm a little hungry. |

| **노랗다** | to be yellow | 잎이 벌써 노랗게 됐어요. |
| | | The leaves have already turned yellow. |

| **훨씬** | much, far | 저는 주말에 훨씬 바빠요. |
| | | I'm much busier on the weekend. |

Let's review!

Complete the story from Day 19 using the words you just learned.

이가 아파서 _____에 갔다.

새로 생긴 치과라서 _____.

의사 선생님이 내 이가 _____ 했다.

조금 _____.

이를 잘 닦는 _____을 기를 것이라고 _____.

이제는 이 닦는 것을 _____ 않을 것이다.

또 선생님은 내 이가 _____ _____ 했다.

그리고 이를 하얗게 만들어 줬다.

_____ 보기 좋아져서 기분이 좋다.

Translation

I had a toothache, so I went to the <u>dentist's office</u>. It was a new dentist's office, so it was <u>neat and tidy</u>. The dentist said I had some <u>decayed</u> teeth. I was a little <u>embarrassed</u>. I <u>made up my mind</u> that I would make a <u>habit</u> of brushing my teeth well. I will not <u>put off</u> brushing my teeth anymore. The dentist also said that my teeth are <u>a little</u> <u>yellow</u>. And she made my teeth white. They look <u>much</u> better, so I feel good.

Word Search – Find 7 words out of the vocabulary you just learned in this chapter.

역	하	두	치	가	약	간
아	결	삼	과	랑	건	심
빈	심	다	노	어	소	미
우	하	역	미	루	다	궁
썩	다	지	라	제	경	루
어	해	깔	다	로	습	권
창	훨	씬	간	은	관	보

Fill in the blanks with Korean words that matches its English translation.

Word bank	
치과	결심하다
깔끔하다	미루다
썩다	약간
창피하다	노랗다
습관	훨씬

01 habit

_____

02 to be clean, to be neat and tidy

_____

03 to decay

_____

04 to be embarrassed, to be ashamed

_____

05 to be yellow

_____

Day 20

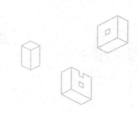

- **기침** ------------------ ⬡
- **빨갛다** ---------------- ⬡
- **온몸** ------------------ ⬡
- **가렵다** ---------------- ⬡
- **해산물** ---------------- ⬡
- **알레르기** -------------- ⬡
- **국물** ------------------ ⬡
- **다행히** ---------------- ⬡
- **증상** ------------------ ⬡
- **사라지다** -------------- ⬡

Day 20 Let's warm up!

....

Imagine the situation in the story below to remember the ten Korean words in context.

오늘 친구랑 저녁을 먹었다.

I had dinner with my friend today.

그런데 갑자기 친구가 **기침**을 하기 시작했다.

And then suddenly my friend started to <u>cough</u>.

기침을 많이 해서 얼굴이 **빨갛게** 됐다.

He coughed so much that his face turned <u>red</u>.

친구는 **온몸**이 너무 **가렵다고** 했다.

My friend told me his <u>whole body</u> was too <u>itchy</u>.

그래서 친구랑 병원에 갔는데 **해산물 알레르기**라고 했다.

So I went to the hospital with my friend, and the doctor said that my friend was <u>allergic</u> to <u>seafood</u>.

우리가 먹은 **국물**에 해산물이 있었나 보다.

I guess there was seafood in the <u>soup</u> that we had.

다행히 약을 먹으니까 **증상**이 **사라졌다**.

<u>Fortunately</u>, after taking medicine, the <u>symptoms</u> <u>disappeared</u>.

Let's keep the ball rolling!

Word	Meaning	Example
기침	cough	저는 매운 걸 먹으면 기침을 해요. When I eat spicy food, I cough.
빨갛다	to be red	당황해서 얼굴이 빨개졌어요. I was embarrassed, so my face turned red.
온몸	whole body	온몸이 아파서 오늘 학교 못 갈 것 같아요. My whole body is in pain, so I can't go to school today.
가렵다	to be itchy	오늘 머리를 못 감아서 머리가 너무 가려워요. I couldn't wash my hair today, so my hair is too itchy.
해산물	seafood	저는 해산물을 별로 안 좋아해요. I don't like seafood much.
알레르기	allergy	알레르기가 있는 사람은 미리 알려주세요. If you have any allergies, please let me know in advance.

| **국물** | soup | 날씨가 추우니까 따뜻한 국물이 먹고 싶어요. |
| | | Since the weather is cold, I want to have warm soup. |

| **다행히** | fortunately | 다행히 지각은 안 했어요. |
| | | Fortunately, I wasn't late. |

| **증상** | symptom | 증상을 자세히 말해 주세요. |
| | | Please describe your symptoms in detail. |

| **사라지다** | to disappear, to go (away) | 약을 먹으니까 통증이 사라졌어요. |
| | | After taking the medicine, the pain disappeared. |

Let's review!

Complete the story from Day 20 using the words you just learned.

오늘 친구랑 저녁을 먹었다.

그런데 갑자기 친구가 _____을 하기 시작했다.

기침을 많이 해서 얼굴이 _____ 됐다.

친구는 _____이 너무 _____ 했다.

그래서 친구랑 병원에 갔는데 _____ _____라고 했다.

우리가 먹은 _____에 해산물이 있었나 보다.

_____ 약을 먹으니까 _____이 _____.

Translation

I had dinner with my friend today. And then suddenly my friend started to <u>cough</u>. He coughed so much that his face turned <u>red</u>. My friend told me his <u>whole body</u> was too <u>itchy</u>. So I went to the hospital with my friend, and the doctor said that my friend was <u>allergic</u> to <u>seafood</u>. I guess there was seafood in the <u>soup</u> that we had. <u>Fortunately</u>, after taking medicine, the <u>symptoms</u> <u>disappeared</u>.

Crossword Puzzle

	01			02		
03					04	
		05				
	06			07		

01 whole body

02 to be red

03 seafood

04 to disappear, to go (away)

05 soup

06 symptom

07 to be itchy

Fill in the blanks with Korean words that matches its English translation.

Word bank	
기침	알레르기
빨갛다	국물
온몸	다행히
가렵다	증상
해산물	사라지다

01 fortunately   _____

02 cough   _____

03 whole body   _____

04 symptom   _____

05 allergy   _____

01 How do you say "yawn" in Korean?

    a. 하루   **b.** 하늘   **c.** 하품   **d.** 하나

02 Which of the following does <u>not</u> become a verb if you attach -하다?

    a. 결심   **b.** 연주   **c.** 당황   **d.** 당장

03 What is the Korean word for the item in the picture? _____

04 Which of the following words is related to a company?

    a. 축제   **b.** 주방   **c.** 회식   **d.** 풍경

05 What is the antonym of 장점? _____

06 What does 베란다 refer to?

    a. outdoor balcony   b. indoor balcony
    c. outdoor window   d. indoor window

07 Which of the following is <u>not</u> good to get?

    a. 벌금   b. 추억   c. 도움   d. 월급

08 What color does your face turn when you are embarrassed or coughing a lot?

    a. 까맣다   b. 노랗다   c. 빨갛다   d. 하얗다

09 Choose the one that is closest in meaning to the underlined word.

잠을 잘 자서 기분이 너무 좋아요. = I feel very good because I slept well.

    a. 좀   b. 푹   c. 꼭   d. 더

10 Which of the following words does <u>not</u> belong to 증상?

    a. 기침   b. 가렵다   c. 알레르기   d. 깔끔하다

[11-20] Fill in the blanks using the words that you learned in Day 11 - Day 20.

11 저는 성격이 _____ 사람이 좋아요.
    = I like people who have an outgoing personality.

12 엄청 큰 _____ 이/가 났어요.
    = I got a really big pimple.

13 식물을 _____ 게 취미예요.
    = Growing plants is my hobby.

14 비행기가 출발하기 전에 _____ 탔어요.
    = I barely got on the airplane before it took off.

15 영화관에서 앞 좌석을 발로 _____ 마세요.
    = Don't kick the seat in front of you in the movie theater.

16 오늘 저녁에 피아노 _____ 가요?
    = Are you going to the piano school tonight?

17 바지에 _____이/가 나서 갈아입었어요.

= My pants got a hole, so I changed them.

18 책상 위에 있는 물건 좀 _____.

= Please organize the stuff on your desk.

19 저는 주말에 _____ 바빠요.

= I'm much busier on the weekend.

20 _____ 지각은 안 했어요.

= Fortunately, I wasn't late.

Day 21

- ⬡ **동료** ----------------------- ⬡
- ⬡ **불만** ----------------------- ⬡
- ⬡ **표정** ----------------------- ⬡
- ⬡ **첫인상** --------------------- ⬡
- ⬡ **고민** ----------------------- ⬡
- ⬡ **상담** ----------------------- ⬡
- ⬡ **평소** ----------------------- ⬡
- ⬡ **곤란하다** ------------------- ⬡
- ⬡ **고치다** --------------------- ⬡
- ⬡ **조언하다** ------------------- ⬡

Day 21

Imagine the situation in the story below to
remember the ten Korean words in context.

내 옆자리 **동료**는 항상 **불만**이 있는 **표정**을 하고 있다.

My <u>co-worker</u> in the seat next to me always has a <u>look</u> of <u>complaint</u>
on her face.

그래서 **첫인상**이 너무 안 좋았다.

So my <u>first impression</u> of her was very bad.

어느 날 동료가 **고민 상담**을 받고 싶다고 했다.

One day, my co-worker said she wanted to get some <u>advice</u> about
her <u>concerns</u>.

동료는 **평소**에 표정이 안 좋아서 **곤란한** 일이 많았다
고 했다.

My co-worker said her <u>usual</u> facial expression is not good, so she
has had many <u>difficult</u> situations.

그래서 표정을 **고치고** 싶다고 했다.

So she said she wanted to <u>fix</u> her facial expression.

나는 웃는 연습을 하라고 **조언했다**.

I <u>advised</u> her to practice smiling.

요즘 동료의 표정이 좋아진 것 같아서 기분이 좋다.

These days it seems like my co-worker's facial expression got
better, so I feel good.

Let's keep the ball rolling!

Word	Meaning	Example
동료	co-worker, colleague	회사 동료들이랑 친해요? Are you close to your co-workers?
불만	complaint, dissatisfaction, problem	왜? 불만 있어? What? Is there a problem?
표정	facial expression, look, face	오늘 표정이 왜 이렇게 안 좋아? Why is your facial expression so bad today?
첫인상	first impression	우리 처음 만났을 때 내 첫인상 어땠어? How was your first impression of me when we met for the first time?
고민	concern, worry	저는 인생에 고민이 별로 없어요. In my life I don't have many concerns.
상담	advice, counsel, consultation	저 연애 상담 좀 해 주세요. Please give me some relationship advice.

| 평소 | usual day, usual times | 오늘은 평소보다 사람이 많네.
Today there are more people than usual. |

평소 usual day, usual times

오늘은 평소보다 사람이 많네.
Today there are more people than usual.

곤란하다 to be difficult, to be embarrassed, to be awkward

그 질문에는 대답하기가 조금 곤란하네요.
It's a difficult question for me to answer.

고치다 to fix, to revise

시계가 멈춰서 고치고 있었어요.
The clock stopped so I was fixing it.

조언하다 to advise

한국어를 잘하고 싶은데 조언 좀 해 주세요.
I want to speak Korean well, so please give me some advice.

Let's review!

Complete the story from Day 21 using the words you just learned.

내 옆자리 _____는 항상 _____이 있는 _____을 하고 있다.

그래서 _____이 너무 안 좋았다.

어느 날 동료가 _____ _____을 받고 싶다고 했다.

동료는 _____에 표정이 안 좋아서 _____ 일이 많았다고 했다.

그래서 표정을 _____ 싶다고 했다.

나는 웃는 연습을 하라고 _____.

요즘 동료의 표정이 좋아진 것 같아서 기분이 좋다.

Translation

My co-worker in the seat next to me always has a look of complaint on her face. So my first impression of her was very bad. One day, my co-worker said she wanted to get some advice about her concerns. My co-worker said her usual facial expression is not good, so she has had many difficult situations. So she said she wanted to fix her facial expression. I advised her to practice smiling. These days it seems like my co-worker's facial expression got better, so I feel good.

Word Search - Find 7 words out of the vocabulary you just learned in this chapter.

동	답	치	고	구	고	민
료	가	계	생	별	치	불
도	언	곤	란	하	다	회
늘	초	다	인	친	때	료
사	대	상	불	만	허	지
희	우	소	고	서	포	코
첫	인	상	점	곤	표	정

Fill in the blanks with Korean words that matches its English translation.

Word bank	
동료	상담
불만	평소
표정	곤란하다
첫인상	고치다
고민	조언하다

01 complaint, dissatisfaction, problem

_____

02 advice, counsel, consultation

_____

03 first impression

_____

04 to advise

_____

05 usual day, usual times

_____

Day 22

- 청소기 ------------- ⬡
- 제품 --------------- ⬡
- 검색하다 ----------- ⬡
- 딱 ----------------- ⬡
- 판매하다 ----------- ⬡
- 퍼센트 ------------- ⬡
- 할인 --------------- ⬡
- 가습기 ------------- ⬡
- 무료 --------------- ⬡
- 환불 --------------- ⬡

Day 22

Let's warm up!

Imagine the situation in the story below to
remember the ten Korean words in context.

청소기를 사야 하는데, 어떤 **제품**을 사는 게 좋을까?

I need to buy a **vacuum cleaner**. Which **product** will be good to buy?

나는 인터넷에 청소기를 **검색했다**.

I **searched** for a vacuum cleaner on the Internet.

첫 번째 청소기는 **딱** 오늘 하루만 9만 9천 원에 **판매하고** 있다.

As for the first vacuum cleaner, they are **selling** it for 99,000 won
just for today.

두 번째 청소기는 20**퍼센트 할인**을 하고 있다.

The second vacuum cleaner, they are offering it with a 20 **percent
discount**.

그 청소기를 사면 **가습기**를 **무료**로 준다고 한다.

If you buy that vacuum cleaner, they said they will give you a
humidifier for **free**.

두 제품 다 **환불**은 안 된다.

For both of those products, a **refund** is not available.

어떤 것을 사야 할까? 정말 고민이다.

Which one should I buy? I really cannot decide.

Let's keep the ball rolling!

Word	Meaning	Example
청소기	vacuum cleaner	얼마 전에 로봇 청소기 샀는데 진짜 편해요. Recently I bought a robot vacuum cleaner and it's really convenient.
제품	product, goods	그 립스틱은 어느 회사 제품이에요? Which company's product is that lipstick?
검색하다	to search, to browse	인터넷에 TTMIK을 검색해 보세요! Search TTMIK on the Internet!
딱	just, exactly, precisely	딱 한 입만 더 먹고 그만 먹을 거야. I'm going to take just one more bite and stop eating.
판매하다	to sell, to merchandise	이번 콘서트 표는 온라인에서만 판매합니다. We sell the tickets for this concert online only.
퍼센트	percent	인간의 몸은 70퍼센트가 물로 이루어져 있습니다. 70 percent of the human body is made up of water.

할인	discount	이번 주까지 TTMIK 도서 할인 기간이에요! It's the TTMIK book discount period until this week!
가습기	humidifier	방이 너무 건조해서 가습기 틀었어. The room was very dry, so I turned on the humidifier.
무료	free of charge, no cost	한복을 입으면 경복궁에 무료로 입장할 수 있어요. If you wear a Han-bok, you can enter Gyeongbok Palace for free.
환불	refund	제품을 구매한 후 7일 안에 환불 가능합니다. After you purchase the product, you can get a refund within 7 days.

Let's review!

Complete the story from Day 22 using the words you just learned.

_____를 사야 하는데, 어떤 _____을 사는 게 좋을까?

나는 인터넷에 청소기를 _____.

첫 번째 청소기는 ___ 오늘 하루만 9만 9천 원에 _____ 있다.

두 번째 청소기는 20_____ _____을 하고 있다.

그 청소기를 사면 _____를 _____로 준다고 한다.

두 제품 다 _____은 안 된다.

어떤 것을 사야 할까? 정말 고민이다.

Translation

I need to buy a **vacuum cleaner**. Which **product** will be good to buy? I **searched** for a vacuum cleaner on the Internet. As for the first vacuum cleaner, they are **selling** it for 99,000 won **just** for today. The second vacuum cleaner, they are offering it with a 20 **percent discount**. If you buy that vacuum cleaner, they said they will give you a **humidifier** for **free**. For both of those products, a **refund** is not available. Which one should I buy? I really cannot decide.

Crossword Puzzle

01		02				
				03		
04						
					05	
	06					
		07				

01 just, exactly, precisely

02 humidifier

03 to search, to browse

04 vacuum cleaner

05 product, goods

06 to sell, to merchandise

07 free of charge, no cost

Fill in the blanks with Korean words that matches its English translation.

Word bank	
청소기	퍼센트
제품	할인
검색하다	가습기
딱	무료
판매하다	환불

01 discount   _____

02 humidifier   _____

03 refund   _____

04 product, goods   _____

05 percent   _____

Day 23

Day 23

Imagine the situation in the story below to remember the ten Korean words in context.

나는 **매주** 네 번 **이상 햄버거**를 먹는다.

I eat **hamburgers** **no less than** four times **every week**.

메뉴판을 보지도 않고 항상 햄버거 **세트**를 주문한다.

I do not even look at the **menu** and always order a hamburger **set**.

오늘도 햄버거 세트를 샀다.

Today, as usual, I bought a hamburger set.

지난번에는 **케첩**이 **모자랐었다**.

Last time I was **short of** **ketchup**.

그래서 이번에는 케첩을 많이 달라고 말했다.

So this time I asked them to give me a lot of ketchup.

집에 와서 보니까 **봉지** 안에 케첩이 **가득** 들어 있었다.

When I got home and looked at it, **the bag** was **full** of ketchup.

오늘은 케첩이 많이 **남을** 것 같다.

I think there will be a lot of ketchup **left over** today.

Let's keep the ball rolling!

Word	Meaning	Example
매주	every week, weekly	저는 매주 토요일마다 등산을 해요. I go hiking every Saturday.
이상	not less than, or more	제 친구는 하루에 5번 이상 커피를 마셔요. My friend drinks coffee five times a day or more.
햄버거	hamburger	어떤 햄버거 주문할까? What kind of hamburger should I order?
메뉴판	menu	여기 메뉴판 좀 주세요. Please give me the menu.
세트	set	회사에서 추석 선물 세트를 받았어요. I got a Chuseok gift set from my company.
케첩	ketchup	나는 감자 튀김을 케첩에 찍어 먹는 걸 좋아해. I like to dip my fries in ketchup.

모자라다	to be short (of), to lack, to be not enough	음식이 모자랄 것 같은데 더 사 올까? I don't think we have enough food. Should I go and buy more?
봉지	bag, sack	이거 봉지에 담아 주세요. Please put this in a bag.
가득	fully	사람들이 식당에 가득 차 있었어요. The restaurant was full of people.
남다	to be left (over), to remain	돈이 얼마 안 남아서 아껴야 해요. I don't have much money left, so I have to save it.

Let's review!

Complete the story from Day 23 using the words you just learned.

나는 _____ 네 번 _____ _____를 먹는다.

_____을 보지도 않고 항상 햄버거 _____를 주문한다.

오늘도 햄버거 세트를 샀다.

지난번에는 _____이 _____.

그래서 이번에는 케첩을 많이 달라고 말했다.

집에 와서 보니까 _____ 안에 케첩이 _____ 들어 있었다.

오늘은 케첩이 많이 _____ 것 같다.

Translation

I eat <u>hamburgers</u> <u>no less than</u> four times <u>every week</u>. I do not even look at the <u>menu</u> and always order a hamburger <u>set</u>. Today, as usual, I bought a hamburger set. Last time I was <u>short of</u> <u>ketchup</u>. So this time I asked them to give me a lot of ketchup. When I got home and looked at it, <u>the bag</u> was <u>full</u> of ketchup. I think there will be a lot of ketchup <u>left over</u> today.

Word Search – Find 7 words out of the vocabulary you just learned in this chapter.

이	상	득	받	트	던	모
추	매	저	회	메	껴	자
등	사	산	피	뉴	담	라
석	문	선	마	판	찍	다
커	햄	버	거	물	어	서
남	다	주	좋	세	모	희
마	튀	가	득	케	봉	지

··

Fill in the blanks with Korean words that matches its English translation.

Word bank	
매주 이상 햄버거 메뉴판 세트	케첩 모자라다 봉지 가득 남다

01 every week, weekly

_____

02 to be short (of), to lack,
    to be not enough

_____

03 set

_____

04 to be left (over), to remain

_____

05 ketchup

_____

Day 24

- 재활용하다 --------------- ⬡
- 가위 ------------------ ⬡
- 자르다 ---------------- ⬡
- 동그랗다 -------------- ⬡
- 단추 ------------------ ⬡
- 얇다 ------------------ ⬡
- 끈 --------------------- ⬡
- 꼬리 -------------------- ⬡
- 세상 ------------------ ⬡
- 완성하다 --------------- ⬡

Day 24

Let's warm up!

Imagine the situation in the story below to remember the ten Korean words in context.

나는 안 쓰는 물건을 **재활용하는** 것을 좋아한다.

I like to <u>recycle</u> things that I do not use.

오늘은 바지로 강아지 인형을 만들었다.

Today I made a stuffed puppy with my pants.

먼저 바지를 **가위**로 **잘랐다**.

First, I <u>cut</u> my pants with <u>scissors</u>.

그것으로 강아지 인형의 얼굴과 몸을 만들었다.

With that, I made the face and body of the stuffed puppy.

동그란 단추로 눈도 만들었다.

With <u>round</u> <u>buttons</u>, I also made the eyes.

안 쓰는 **얇은 끈**으로 **꼬리**도 만들었다.

I also made a <u>tail</u> with a <u>thin</u> <u>strap</u> that I do not use.

세상에 하나밖에 없는 강아지 인형을 **완성했다**.

I <u>completed</u> a stuffed puppy that is the only one of its kind in the <u>world</u>.

Let's keep the ball rolling!

Word	Meaning	Example
재활용하다	to recycle	플라스틱병이나 유리병을 재활용할 수 있어요. You can recycle plastic bottles or glass bottles.
가위	scissors	거기 있는 가위 좀 주세요. Please give me the scissors over there.
자르다	to cut	머리를 짧게 잘랐어요. I cut my hair short.
동그랗다	to be round	그 여자는 얼굴이 동그래요. She has a round face.
단추	button	너 셔츠 단추 잘못 채웠어. You buttoned your shirt wrong.
얇다	to be thin	옷이 너무 얇아서 추워요. My clothes are too thin so I feel cold.

끈	string, strap, lace	운동화 끈이 풀어져서 넘어질 뻔했어. I almost fell down because my shoelace came loose.
꼬리	tail	고양이가 꼬리를 흔들고 있어요. The cat is wagging its tail.
세상	world	나는 세상에서 우리 엄마가 제일 좋아. I like my mother the most in the world.
완성하다	to complete	그 작가는 30년 만에 이 소설을 완성했습니다. The author completed this novel in 30 years.

Let's review!

Complete the story from Day 24 using the words you just learned.

나는 안 쓰는 물건을 _____ 것을 좋아한다.

오늘은 바지로 강아지 인형을 만들었다.

먼저 바지를 _____로 _____.

그것으로 강아지 인형의 얼굴과 몸을 만들었다.

_____ _____로 눈도 만들었다.

안 쓰는 _____ ___으로 _____도 만들었다.

_____에 하나밖에 없는 강아지 인형을 _____.

Translation

I like to <u>recycle</u> things that I do not use. Today I made a stuffed puppy with my pants. First, I <u>cut</u> my pants with <u>scissors</u>. With that, I made the face and body of the stuffed puppy. With <u>round</u> <u>buttons</u>, I also made the eyes. I also made a <u>tail</u> with a <u>thin</u> <u>strap</u> that I do not use. I <u>completed</u> a stuffed puppy that is the only one of its kind in the <u>world</u>.

Crossword Puzzle

		01				
02			03			
	04		05			
				06		
				07		

01 to be thin

02 to cut

03 button

04 tail

05 to complete

06 world

07 scissors

Fill in the blanks with Korean words that matches its English translation.

Word bank	
재활용하다	얇다
가위	끈
자르다	꼬리
동그랗다	세상
단추	완성하다

01 to be round _____

02 to complete _____

03 scissors _____

04 to recycle _____

05 string, strap, lace _____

Day 25

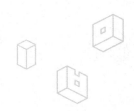

Day 25

Let's warm up!

....

Imagine the situation in the story below to remember the ten Korean words in context.

학교 **게시판**에서 **골프** 대회 **광고**를 봤다.

On the school **bulletin board**, I saw an **advertisement** for a **golf** tournament.

사실 나는 전부터 골프 대회에 **참가해** 보고 싶었다.

Actually, I have always wanted to **participate** in a golf tournament.

광고를 보니까 **선수 모집** 기간이 얼마 남지 않았었다.

Based on the advertisement, there was not much time left in the **player** **recruitment** period.

나는 **급하게** 참가 **신청서**를 제출했다.

I **urgently** submitted an **application** for participation.

그런데 대회 날 선수 **목록**에 내 이름이 없었다.

But on the day of the tournament, my name was not on the **list** of players.

내가 실수로 **볼링** 대회에 신청서를 낸 것이었다.

By mistake, I had submitted the application for a **bowling** tournament.

Let's keep the ball rolling!

Word	Meaning	Example
게시판	bulletin board, noticeboard	파일은 온라인 게시판에 올려 주세요. Please post the file on the online bulletin board.
골프	golf	아빠는 골프 치러 가셨어요. Dad went to play golf.
광고	advertisement, commercial	저 사람 저 광고에 나오는 모델 아니야? Isn't she the model in that commercial?
참가하다	to participate	마라톤에 참가하시는 분들은 운동장으로 모여 주세요. If you're participating in the marathon, please gather in the playground.
선수	player, athlete	저는 커서 야구 선수가 되고 싶어요. When I grow up, I want to be a baseball player.
모집	recruitment	신입생 모집은 언제부터 시작해요? When does the recruitment for the new students start?

급하다	to be urgent, to be in a hurry	밥을 급하게 먹어서 배가 아파요. I ate in a hurry, so my stomach hurts.
신청서	application	신청서를 작성해 주세요. Please fill out the application form.
목록	list, table	내 통화 목록에는 엄마랑 아빠밖에 없어. On my call list, there is only my mom and dad.
볼링	bowling	저 지난주부터 볼링 시작했어요. I started bowling last week.

Let's review!

Complete the story from Day 25 using the words you just learned.

학교 _____에서 _____ 대회 _____를 봤다.

사실 나는 전부터 골프 대회에 _____ 보고 싶었다.

광고를 보니까 _____ _____ 기간이 얼마 남지 않았었다.

나는 _____ 참가 _____를 제출했다.

그런데 대회 날 선수 _____에 내 이름이 없었다.

내가 실수로 _____ 대회에 신청서를 낸 것이었다.

Translation

On the school <u>bulletin board</u>, I saw an <u>advertisement</u> for a <u>golf</u> tournament. Actually, I have always wanted to <u>participate</u> in a golf tournament. Based on the advertisement, there was not much time left in the <u>player</u> <u>recruitment</u> period. I <u>urgently</u> submitted an <u>application</u> for participation. But on the day of the tournament, my name was not on the <u>list</u> of players. By mistake, I had submitted the application for a <u>bowling</u> tournament.

Word Search – Find 7 words out of the vocabulary you just learned in this chapter.

광	고	얼	교	남	보	볼
학	마	집	골	게	시	판
조	야	목	푸	하	회	성
구	고	록	대	참	급	숭
기	통	줍	참	가	하	다
빠	전	혜	파	모	다	게
모	집	불	총	신	청	서

Fill in the blanks with Korean words that matches its English translation.

Word bank	
게시판	모집
골프	급하다
광고	신청서
참가하다	목록
선수	볼링

01 bowling   _____

02 to participate   _____

03 list, table   _____

04 player, athlete   _____

05 golf   _____

Day 26

Day 26

....

Imagine the situation in the story below to
remember the ten Korean words in context.

여름에는 음식물을 밖에 **두면** 금방 **상한다**.

In the summer, if you **put food** outside, it **goes bad** quickly.

그래서 꼭 냉장고에 **보관해야** 한다.

So you must **keep** it in the refrigerator.

그런데 냉장고 안에서도 음식물이 상할 수 있다.

However, food can go bad even in the refrigerator.

먼저, **뚜껑**을 잘 **덮지** 않으면 상할 수 있다.

First, if you do not **cover** the **lid** well, it can be spoiled.

그리고 음식물이 **얼었다가 녹았을** 때도 위험하다.

And it is also dangerous when food **freezes** and then **thaws**.

만약 냄새나 색깔이 이상하면, 그 음식은 **이미** 상한 것이다.

If the smell or color is strange, the food is **already** spoiled.

Let's keep the ball rolling!

Word	Meaning	Example
음식물	food and drink, food	음식물 쓰레기는 이쪽에 버려 주세요. Please put the food waste here.
두다	to put, to set, to place	종이랑 연필은 책상 위에 뒀어요. I put the paper and pencil on the desk.
상하다	to go bad, to spoil	그거 상했으니까 먹지 마. It has gone bad, so don't eat it.
보관하다	to keep, to store	가방은 여기에 보관하면 됩니다. You can keep your bag here.
뚜껑	cover, cap, lid	뚜껑이 열려서 커피가 쏟아졌어요. The lid opened and coffee spilled.
덮다	to cover	추우니까 이불 잘 덮고 자야 해. It's cold, so you have to cover yourself with a blanket when you sleep.

| 얼다 | to freeze, to be frozen | 너무 추워서 손이 얼 것 같아요. |
| | | It's so cold that I feel like my hands will freeze. |

| 녹다 | to melt to thaw | 얼음이 녹으면 물이 됩니다. |
| | | When ice melts, it becomes water. |

| 만약 | if, in case | 만약 옷이 안 맞으면 환불할 수 있을까요? |
| | | If the clothes don't fit, can I get a refund? |

| 이미 | already | 이미 늦었으니까 천천히 가자. |
| | | We're already late, so let's go slowly. |

Let's review!

Complete the story from Day 26 using the words you just learned.

여름에는 _____을 밖에 ____ 금방 _____.

그래서 꼭 냉장고에 _____ 한다.

그런데 냉장고 안에서도 음식물이 상할 수 있다.

먼저, ____을 잘 ____ 않으면 상할 수 있다.

그리고 음식물이 _____ _____ 때도 위험하다.

_____ 냄새나 색깔이 이상하면, 그 음식은 _____ 상한 것이다.

Translation

In the summer, if you **put food** outside, it **goes bad** quickly. So you must **keep** it in the refrigerator. However, food can go bad even in the refrigerator. First, if you do not **cover** the **lid** well, it can be spoiled. And it is also dangerous when food **freezes** and then **thaws**. **If** the smell or color is strange, the food is **already** spoiled.

Crossword Puzzle

01			02	

01 cover, cap, lid

02 to go bad, to spoil

03 to keep, to store

04 if, in case

05 to cover

06 already

07 food and drink, food

Fill in the blanks with Korean words that matches its English translation.

Word bank	
음식물	덮다
두다	얼다
상하다	녹다
보관하다	만약
뚜껑	이미

01 to melt, to thaw

_____

02 to freeze, to be frozen

_____

03 if, in case

_____

04 to put, to set, to place

_____

05 food and drink, food

_____

Day 27

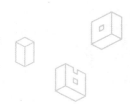

⬡ **패션** ------------------- ◯

⬡ **유행하다** ------------------- ◯

⬡ **파랗다** ------------------- ◯

⬡ **셔츠** ------------------- ◯

⬡ **검다** ------------------- ◯

⬡ **가죽** ------------------- ◯

⬡ **살펴보다** ------------------- ◯

⬡ **상태** ------------------- ◯

⬡ **튼튼하다** ------------------- ◯

⬡ **자랑하다** ------------------- ◯

Day 27

Let's warm up!

Imagine the situation in the story below to
remember the ten Korean words in context.

요즘 2000년대 **패션**이 다시 **유행하고** 있다.

These days, <u>fashion</u> from the 2000s <u>is trending</u> again.

특히 **파란 셔츠**와 **검은 가죽** 치마가 유행이다.

Especially, <u>blue</u> <u>shirts</u> and <u>black</u> <u>leather</u> skirts are in fashion.

나도 사려고 했는데 엄마가 그런 옷들을 가지고 있었다.

I was going to buy some too, but my mom had such clothes.

옷을 **살펴봤는데** 생각보다 **상태**가 좋았다.

I <u>looked at</u> the clothes and they were in better <u>condition</u> than I
thought.

20년 전 옷들인데 아직 **튼튼했다**.

They were clothes from 20 years ago, but they were still <u>strong</u>.

친구들한테 빨리 **자랑하고** 싶다.

I cannot wait to <u>show</u> them to my friends.

Let's keep the ball rolling!

Word	Meaning	Example
패션	fashion, style	저희 언니가 패션 디자이너예요. My older sister is a fashion designer.
유행하다	to be in fashion, to be trending, to be popular	이거 요즘 유행하는 노래인데 들어 볼래? It's a popular song these days. Do you want to listen to it?
파랗다	to be blue	오늘 하늘이 정말 파랗지요? The sky is really blue today, right?
셔츠	shirt	셔츠에 커피가 묻었어요. I have a coffee stain on my shirt.
검다	to be black	제 옷장에는 검은 옷밖에 없어요. In my closet, there are only black clothes.
가죽	leather	아빠께 생일 선물로 가죽 장갑을 드렸어요. I gave my dad leather gloves as a birthday gift.

살펴보다	to look around (in detail), to check (for something)	네가 부엌을 살펴보는 동안, 나는 거실을 살펴볼게. While you look around in the kitchen, I'll look in the living room.
상태	condition, state	그 음식은 상태가 안 좋아서 버려야 돼. I should throw that food away because it's not in good condition.
튼튼하다	to be strong, to be sturdy	나는 다리가 튼튼해서 오래 서 있을 수 있어. My legs are strong so I can stand for a long time.
자랑하다	to show off, to boast	새로 산 가방을 친구들 앞에서 자랑할 거예요. I'm going to show off my new bag in front of my friends.

Let's review!

Complete the story from Day 27 using the words you just learned.

요즘 2000년대 _____이 다시 _____ 있다.

특히 ____ ____와 ____ ____ 치마가 유행이다.

나도 사려고 했는데 엄마가 그런 옷들을 가지고 있었다.

옷을 _____ 생각보다 ____가 좋았다.

20년 전 옷들인데 아직 _____.

친구들한테 빨리 _____ 싶다.

Translation

These days, **fashion** from the 2000s **is trending** again. Especially, **blue** **shirts** and **black** **leather** skirts are in fashion. I was going to buy some too, but my mom had such clothes. I **looked at** the clothes and they were in better **condition** than I thought. They were clothes from 20 years ago, but they were still **strong**. I cannot wait to **show** them to my friends.

....

Word Search – Find 7 words out of the vocabulary you just learned in this chapter.

상	음	파	자	션	랑	상
나	다	라	랑	본	감	태
자	튼	튼	하	다	단	책
거	버	태	다	수	유	어
가	죽	튼	상	죽	행	삼
희	패	유	츠	팔	하	미
파	랗	다	티	검	다	셔

....

Fill in the blanks with Korean words that matches its English translation.

Word bank	
패션 유행하다 파랗다 셔츠 검다	가죽 살펴보다 상태 튼튼하다 자랑하다

01 to be strong, to be sturdy

_____

02 to look around (in detail),
      to check (for something)

_____

03 to show off, to boast

_____

04 fashion, style

_____

05 shirt

_____

Day 28

⬡ **교통사고** ⬡

⬡ **큰길** ⬡

⬡ **인도** ⬡

⬡ **맞은편** ⬡

⬡ **도로** ⬡

⬡ **우회전** ⬡

⬡ **좌회전** ⬡

⬡ **살짝** ⬡

⬡ **깨지다** ⬡

⬡ **신고하다** ⬡

Day 28

Imagine the situation in the story below to
remember the ten Korean words in context.

어제 **교통사고**가 나는 것을 봤다.

I saw a <u>car accident</u> take place yesterday.

나는 **큰길** 옆 **인도**를 걸어가고 있었다.

I was walking on the <u>sidewalk</u> next to the <u>main road</u>.

그때 **맞은편 도로**에 있는 차가 갑자기 **우회전**을
했다.

Then a car on the <u>opposite side</u> of the <u>road</u> suddenly <u>turned right</u>.

그래서 **좌회전**하는 차와 부딪쳤다.

So the car bumped into a car <u>turning left</u>.

그 차 창문이 **살짝 깨진** 것 같았다.

It looked like the window of that car was <u>slightly</u> <u>broken</u>.

나는 빨리 119에 **신고했다**.

I <u>called</u> 119 quickly.

Let's keep the ball rolling!

Word	Meaning	Example
교통사고	traffic accident, car crash	저는 14살 때 교통사고로 조금 다쳤어요. When I was 14 years old, I was slightly injured in a car accident.
큰길	main road	골목길은 어두우니까 밤에는 큰길로 가. It's dark in the alley, so go through the main street at night.
인도	sidewalk	인도에 주차하지 마세요. Don't park on the sidewalk.
맞은편	opposite side, across from	맞은편에 앉은 여자가 자꾸 나를 쳐다봐. The woman sitting across from me keeps looking at me.
도로	road, highway	도로 한가운데에 강아지가 있어! There's a puppy in the middle of the road!
우회전	right turn	은행에서 우회전하면 바로 우리 집이야. If you make a right turn at the bank, my house is right there.

좌회전	left turn	여기서 좌회전해 주세요. Turn left here, please.
살짝	slightly	제가 살짝 미니까 문이 활짝 열렸어요. I pushed the door slightly and it opened wide.
깨지다	to break, to be broken	접시가 바닥에 떨어져서 깨졌어요. The plate fell on the floor and broke.
신고하다	to report, to call	어떤 사람들이 싸우고 있어서 경찰서에 신고했어요. Some people were fighting, so I called the police.

Let's review!

Complete the story from Day 28 using the words you just learned.

어제 _____가 나는 것을 봤다.

나는 _____ 옆 _____를 걸어가고 있었다.

그때 _____ _____에 있는 차가 갑자기 _____을 했다.

그래서 _____하는 차와 부딪쳤다.

그 차 창문이 _____ _____ 것 같았다.

나는 빨리 119에 _____.

Translation

I saw a <u>car accident</u> take place yesterday. I was walking on the <u>sidewalk</u> next to the <u>main road</u>. Then a car on the <u>opposite side</u> of the <u>road</u> suddenly <u>turned right</u>. So the car bumped into a car <u>turning left</u>. It looked like the window of that car was <u>slightly broken</u>. I <u>called</u> 119 quickly.

Crossword Puzzle

01					02	
				03		
04						
				05 ↓		
				06→		
07						

01　traffic accident, car crash

02　left turn

03　right turn

04　to report, to call

05　sidewalk

06　road, highway

07　to break, to be broken

Fill in the blanks with Korean words that matches its English translation.

Word bank	
교통사고	우회전
큰길	좌회전
인도	살짝
맞은편	깨지다
도로	신고하다

01　slightly　_____

02　to break, to be broken　_____

03　opposite side, across from　_____

04　main road　_____

05　traffic accident, car crash　_____

Day 29

Day 29

Imagine the situation in the story below to remember the ten Korean words in context.

어제 한 뉴스 **기사**를 보았다.

I saw a news **article** yesterday.

사람들이 버리는 **가전제품**의 **양**이 **심각하게** 많다고 한다.

It is said that the **amount** of **household appliances** people throw away is **seriously** large.

나도 가전제품이 **고장** 나면 **그냥** 버렸었다.

When my household appliances **break down**, I used to **just** throw them away.

하지만 이제는 고쳐서 더 오래 쓸 것이다.

But from now on, I will fix them and use them longer.

그리고 **새로운** 제품을 사는 대신 **중고** 제품을 살 것이다.

And instead of buying **new** products, I will buy **used products**.

그렇게 하면 **자연**을 더 잘 **보호할** 수 있을 것이다.

By doing so, I will be able to **protect** **nature** better.

Let's keep the ball rolling!

Word	Meaning	Example
기사	article, news	재미있는 기사가 있는데 읽어 볼래? There's an interesting article. Do you want to read it?
가전제품	home appliance, household electrical appliance	냉장고, 텔레비전, 세탁기 같은 것을 다 가전제품이라고 불러. Refrigerators, televisions, and washing machines are all called home appliances.
양	amount	음식을 주문했는데 생각보다 양이 많아요. I ordered food, but the amount of food is bigger than I thought.
심각하다	to be serious, to be severe	요즘 바다 오염이 정말 심각하다고 합니다. I heard that sea pollution is very serious these days.
고장	breakdown, out of order	엘리베이터가 또 고장이야? Is the elevator out of order again?
그냥	just	난 계란에 케첩 안 뿌리고 그냥 먹어. I eat my eggs without putting ketchup on them.

새롭다

to be new

그 회사는 새로운 상품을 개발하고 있습니다.

The company is developing a new product.

중고

used product

이 피아노는 중고지만 깨끗하고 소리도 잘 나.

This piano is a used one, but it's clean and sounds good.

자연

nature

도시도 좋지만 저는 자연을 더 좋아해요.

I like cities, too, but I prefer nature more.

보호하다

to protect

1시간에 한 번씩 눈을 쉬면 시력을 보호할 수 있어요.

If you rest your eyes once every hour, you can protect your eyesight.

Let's review!

Complete the story from Day 29 using the words you just learned.

어제 한 뉴스 _____ 를 보았다.

사람들이 버리는 _____의 ___이 _____ 많다고 한다.

나도 가전제품이 _____ 나면 _____ 버렸었다.

하지만 이제는 고쳐서 더 오래 쓸 것이다.

그리고 _____ 제품을 사는 대신 _____ 제품을 살 것이다.

그렇게 하면 _____을 더 잘 _____ 수 있을 것이다.

Translation

I saw a news <u>article</u> yesterday. It is said that the <u>amount</u> of <u>household appliances</u> people throw away is <u>seriously</u> large. When my household appliances <u>break down</u>, I used to <u>just</u> throw them away. But from now on, I will fix them and use them longer. And instead of buying <u>new</u> products, I will buy <u>used products</u>. By doing so, I will be able to <u>protect</u> <u>nature</u> better.

Word Search - Find 7 words out of the vocabulary you just learned in this chapter.

보	호	하	다	야	새	심
수	시	케	재	텔	란	각
가	것	그	계	타	바	하
전	장	냥	자	오	냉	다
제	도	력	전	중	마	미
품	보	쉬	호	고	장	서
사	새	롭	다	염	리	기

Fill in the blanks with Korean words that matches its English translation.

Word bank	
기사	그냥
가전제품	새롭다
양	중고
심각하다	자연
고장	보호하다

01 amount

_____

02 to be serious, to be severe

_____

03 to protect

_____

04 nature

_____

05 article, news

_____

Day 30

⬡ **입학시험** ------------------ ⬡

⬡ **학과** ------------------ ⬡

⬡ **합격하다** ------------------ ⬡

⬡ **등록금** ------------------ ⬡

⬡ **놀이공원** ------------------ ⬡

⬡ **늘** ------------------ ⬡

⬡ **등** ------------------ ⬡

⬡ **놓치다** ------------------ ⬡

⬡ **결국** ------------------ ⬡

⬡ **기업** ------------------ ⬡

Day 30

Let's warm up!

Imagine the situation in the story below to remember the ten Korean words in context.

나는 대학교 **입학시험**을 열심히 준비했다.
I prepared hard for the college **entrance exam**.

그래서 내가 원하는 **학과**에 지원했고 **합격했다**.
So I applied for the **major** that I wanted and I **passed**.

하지만 **등록금**을 낼 돈이 없었다.
But I did not have the money to pay the **tuition**.

그래서 평일에는 학원에서 일하고 주말에는 **놀이공원**에서 일했다.
So I worked at a private academy on weekdays and at an **amusement park** on weekends.

정말 바빴지만 **늘** 열심히 공부해서 1**등**을 **놓치지** 않았다.
I was really busy, but I **always** studied hard so I did not **miss** getting first **place** in class.

결국 지금은 좋은 **기업**에서 일을 하고 있다.
As a result, now I am working for a good **company**.

Let's keep the ball rolling!

Word	Meaning	Example
입학시험	entrance examination	요즘 난 고등학교 입학시험을 준비 중이야. These days, I'm preparing for the high school entrance exam.
학과	major, department	저희 학과에는 남학생보다 여학생이 훨씬 많아요. In our department, there are many more female students than male students.
합격하다	to pass, to get accepted	엄마, 나 그 회사에 합격했어! Mom, I got accepted into the company!
등록금	tuition, school expenses	다음 학기 등록금 벌려면 방학 동안 열심히 일해야 돼. To earn tuition for the next semester, I have to work hard during the vacation.
놀이공원	amusement park	마지막으로 놀이공원에 간 게 언제야? When was the last time you went to an amusement park?
늘	always, the whole time	그 사람 책상은 늘 깨끗해. His desk is always clean.

등	rank, place	너 이번 시험에서 몇 등 했어? What was your rank on this test?
놓치다	to miss, to lose	이번 대회에서 금메달을 놓쳐서 너무 슬퍼요. I missed getting the gold medal in this competition, so I'm very sad.
결국	eventually, after all, as a result	남자 친구랑 맨날 싸워서 결국 헤어졌어. I fought with my boyfriend every day, so eventually we broke up.
기업	company, enterprise	이 기업은 20년 전에 설립되었습니다. This company was established 20 years ago.

Let's review!

Complete the story from Day 30 using the words you just learned.

나는 대학교 _____을 열심히 준비했다.

그래서 내가 원하는 _____에 지원했고 _____.

하지만 _____을 낼 돈이 없었다.

그래서 평일에는 학원에서 일하고 주말에는 _____에서 일했다.

정말 바빴지만 ____ 열심히 공부해서 1____을 _____ 않았다.

_____ 지금은 좋은 _____에서 일을 하고 있다.

Translation

I prepared hard for the college <u>entrance exam</u>. So I applied for the <u>major</u> that I wanted and I <u>passed</u>. But I did not have the money to pay the <u>tuition</u>. So I worked at a private academy on weekdays and at an <u>amusement park</u> on weekends. I was really busy, but I <u>always</u> studied hard so I did not <u>miss</u> getting first <u>place</u> in class. <u>As a result</u>, now I am working for a good <u>company</u>.

Crossword Puzzle

		01			02	
03						
		04				05
	06					
		07				

01 tuition, school expenses

02 amusement park

03 eventually, after all, as a result

04 major, department

05 to miss, to lose

06 company, enterprise

07 to pass, to get accepted

Fill in the blanks with Korean words that matches its English translation.

Word bank	
입학시험	늘
학과	등
합격하다	놓치다
등록금	결국
놀이공원	기업

01 rank, place _____

02 eventually, after all, as a result _____

03 entrance examination _____

04 to pass, to get accepted _____

05 always, the whole time _____

01 Choose the word that is <u>not</u> an edible item.

    a. 햄버거   **b.** 케첩   **c.** 단추   **d.** 음식물

02 How do you say "humidifier" in Korean?

    a. 청소기   **b.** 가습기   **c.** 가전제품   **d.** 가죽

03 What is the Korean word for the item in the picture? _____

04 Which of the following words is <u>not</u> related to clothes?

    a. 셔츠   **b.** 치마   **c.** 스타킹   **d.** 자연

05 What is the antonym of 얼다? _____

06 Choose a word which is <u>not</u> related to sports.

  a. 골프   b. 고장   c. 선수   d. 볼링

07 How do you say "used product" in Korean? _____

08 Write the character that can fit in all of the blanks. _____

모____라다	____르다	____연
= to be not enough	= to cut	= nature

09 Which of the following words is <u>not</u> related to school?

  a. 학과   b. 도로   c. 등록금   d. 입학시험

10 What does 게시판 refer to?

  a. white board   b. key board
  c. bulletin board   d. skate board

11 오늘 _____이/가 왜 이렇게 안 좋아?

= Why is your facial expression so bad today?

12 오늘은 _____보다 사람이 많네.

= Today there are more people than usual.

13 인터넷에 TTMIK을 _____ 보세요!

= Search TTMIK on the Internet!

14 이거 _____에 담아 주세요.

= Please put this in a bag.

15 그거 _____ 먹지 마.

= It has gone bad, so don't eat it.

16 제가 _____ 미니까 문이 활짝 열렸어요.

= I pushed the door slightly and it opened wide.

17 나는 다리가 _____ 오래 서 있을 수 있어.

= My legs are strong, so I can stand for a long time.

18 이 _____은/는 20년 전에 설립되었습니다.

= This company was established 20 years ago.

19 마지막으로 _____에 간 게 언제야?

= When was the last time you went to an amusement park?

20 한복을 입으면 경복궁에 _____로 입장할 수 있어요.

= If you wear a Han-bok, you can enter Gyeongbok Palace for free.

QUIZ

DAY 21-30

Day 31

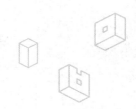

- 막내 ----------------------- ○
- 자꾸 ----------------------- ○
- 뺏다 ----------------------- ○
- 도망가다 ------------------- ○
- 꽉 -------------------------- ○
- 멍 -------------------------- ○
- 혼나다 ----------------------- ○
- 얼른 ------------------------ ○
- 사과하다 --------------------- ○
- 화해하다 --------------------- ○

Day 31

Let's warm up!

....

Imagine the situation in the story below to remember the ten Korean words in context.

공부를 하고 있었는데 **막내** 동생이 **자꾸** 방해했다.

I was studying when my <u>youngest sister</u> <u>kept</u> interrupt<u>ing</u> me.

내 책을 **뺏어서** 자기 방으로 **도망갔다**.

She <u>took</u> my book and <u>ran away</u> to her room.

나는 동생의 팔을 **꽉** 잡고 다시 책을 뺏었다.

I grabbed my younger sister's arm <u>tightly</u> and took my book back from her.

그런데 너무 세게 잡아서 동생 팔에 **멍**이 생겼다.

But I grabbed it too hard, so my younger sister got a <u>bruise</u> on her arm.

엄마한테 **혼날** 것 같아서 **얼른** 사과했다.

I thought I might <u>get scolded</u> by mom, so I <u>quickly</u> <u>apologized</u>.

동생이 사과를 받아 줘서 우리는 **화해했다**.

My younger sister accepted the apology, so we <u>made up</u>.

Let's keep the ball rolling!

Word	Meaning	Example
막내	the youngest (of the family)	막내는 아직 유치원에 다녀요. My youngest brother/sister is still attending kindergarten.
자꾸	repeatedly, again and again	요즘 자꾸 해야 할 일을 잊어버려요. These days, I repeatedly forget what I have to do.
뺏다	to take away	어젯밤에 엄마가 제 핸드폰을 뺏어 갔어요. My mom took away my cell phone last night.
도망가다	to run away	도망가다가 넘어졌어요. As I was running away, I fell down.
꽉	tightly	손잡이 꽉 잡아요. Hold on to the handle tightly.
멍	bruise	넘어져서 무릎에 멍이 생겼어요. I fell down, so I got a bruise on my knee.

혼나다	to get a scolding	오늘 학교에서 선생님한테 혼났어요. Today, I got scolded by my teacher at school.
얼른	quickly	식기 전에 얼른 먹어요. Eat quickly before it gets cold.
사과하다	to apologize	먼저 사과하는 사람이 이기는 거야. Whoever apologizes first wins.
화해하다	to make up, to make peace with	이제 화해할 때 되지 않았어? Isn't it about time you made up?

Let's review!

Complete the story from Day 31 using the words you just learned.

공부를 하고 있었는데 ＿＿＿＿ 동생이 ＿＿＿＿ 방해했다.

내 책을 ＿＿＿＿＿ 자기 방으로 ＿＿＿＿＿＿＿.

나는 동생의 팔을 ＿＿ 잡고 다시 책을 뺏었다.

그런데 너무 세게 잡아서 동생 팔에 ＿＿＿이 생겼다.

엄마한테 ＿＿＿＿ 것 같아서 ＿＿＿＿ ＿＿＿＿＿＿＿.

동생이 사과를 받아 줘서 우리는 ＿＿＿＿＿＿＿.

Translation

I was studying when my <u>youngest sister</u> <u>kept</u> interrup<u>ting</u> me. She <u>took</u> my book and <u>ran away</u> to her room. I grabbed my younger sister's arm <u>tightly</u> and took my book back from her. But I grabbed it too hard, so my younger sister got a <u>bruise</u> on her arm. I thought I might <u>get scolded</u> by mom, so I <u>quickly</u> <u>apologized</u>. My younger sister accepted the apology, so we <u>made up</u>.

Word Search - Find 7 words out of the vocabulary you just learned in this chapter.

꿱	넷	지	희	사	이	교
경	자	꾸	우	과	수	혼
도	고	종	경	하	마	나
얼	효	스	뺏	다	과	다
른	인	하	해	준	얼	현
학	볼	안	우	막	내	소
도	망	가	다	나	드	연

Fill in the blanks with Korean words that matches its English translation.

Word bank	
막내	멍
자꾸	혼나다
뺏다	얼른
도망가다	사과하다
꽉	화해하다

01 tightly _____

02 to apologize _____

03 to make up, to make peace with _____

04 bruise _____

05 to take away _____

Day 32

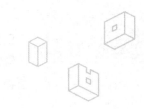

⬡ **삼겹살** ------------------ ⬡

⬡ **김치찌개** -------------- ⬡

⬡ **굽다** ---------------------- ⬡

⬡ **된장** ---------------------- ⬡

⬡ **치우다** ------------------ ⬡

⬡ **귀찮다** ------------------ ⬡

⬡ **몰래** ---------------------- ⬡

⬡ **숨다** ---------------------- ⬡

⬡ **역시** ---------------------- ⬡

⬡ **낫다** ---------------------- ⬡

Day 32

Let's warm up!

Imagine the situation in the story below to
remember the ten Korean words in context.

오늘 우리 가족은 집에서 **삼겹살**과 **김치찌개**를
먹었다.

Today, my family ate <u>grilled pork belly</u> and <u>kimchi stew</u> at home.

오빠가 고기를 **구웠다**.

My older brother <u>grilled</u> the meat.

나는 나가서 **된장**을 사 왔다.

I went out and got <u>soybean paste</u>.

저녁을 다 먹으니까 **치우기**가 너무 **귀찮았다**.

After finishing dinner, I felt too <u>lazy</u> to <u>clean</u> it <u>up</u>.

그래서 나는 **몰래** 방에 **숨었다**.

So, I <u>secretly</u> <u>hid</u> in my room.

역시 집에서 요리하면 할 일이 많다.

<u>As expected</u>, there is a lot to do if we cook at home.

앞으로는 외식을 하는 게 **나을** 것 같다.

I think from now on, eating out will be <u>better</u>.

Let's keep the ball rolling!

Word	Meaning	Example
삼겹살	grilled pork belly	일주일에 한 번은 삼겹살을 먹는 것 같아요. I think I eat grilled pork belly about once a week.
김치찌개	kimchi stew	저는 김치찌개에 돼지고기 넣는 걸 좋아해요. I like putting pork in kimchi stew.
굽다	to grill	야채도 좀 구워 주세요. Please grill some vegetables, too.
된장	soybean paste	된장을 너무 많이 넣은 것 같아요. I think you put in too much soybean paste.
치우다	to clean up	이걸 언제 다 치워요? When will we clean all this up?
귀찮다	to be[feel] lazy, to be a hassle, cannot be bothered to do something	씻기 너무 귀찮아서 그냥 잤어요. I was too lazy to wash up, so I just slept.

몰래	secretly, without other people's knowledge	어렸을 때 엄마 몰래 게임 많이 했어요. When I was little, I played a lot of games without my mom knowing.
숨다	to hide	너무 창피해서 숨고 싶었어요. I was so embarrassed that I wanted to hide.
역시	as expected, as always	역시 이번에도 여행 가서 돈을 많이 썼어요. As expected, I spent a lot of money when I traveled this time, too.
낫다	to be better	인터넷으로 사는 게 더 나아요. It's better to buy it on the Internet.

Let's review!

Complete the story from Day 32 using the words you just learned.

오늘 우리 가족은 집에서 _____과 _____를 먹었다.

오빠가 고기를 _____.

나는 나가서 _____을 사 왔다.

저녁을 다 먹으니까 _____가 너무 _____.

그래서 나는 _____ 방에 _____.

_____ 집에서 요리하면 할 일이 많다.

앞으로는 외식을 하는 게 _____ 것 같다.

Translation

Today, my family ate <u>grilled pork belly</u> and <u>kimchi stew</u> at home.
My older brother <u>grilled</u> the meat. I went out and got <u>soybean
paste</u>. After finishing dinner, I felt too <u>lazy</u> to <u>clean</u> it <u>up</u>. So, I
<u>secretly</u> <u>hid</u> in my room. <u>As expected</u>, there is a lot to do if we cook
at home. I think from now on, eating out will be <u>better</u>.

Crossword Puzzle

	01						
			02				
					03		
04			05				
		06					
				07			

01 to grill
02 to clean up
03 grilled pork belly
04 to hide
05 kimchi stew
06 to be better
07 soybean paste

Fill in the blanks with Korean words that matches its English translation.

Word bank	
삼겹살	귀찮다
김치찌개	몰래
굽다	숨다
된장	역시
치우다	낫다

01 as expected, as always   _____

02 to grill   _____

03 secretly, without other people's knowledge   _____

04 to be[feel] lazy, to be a hassle,
    cannot be bothered to do something   _____

05 to hide   _____

Day 33

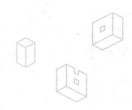

- 체력 ------------------- ⬡
- 관리하다 ------------- ⬡
- 한동안 ---------------- ⬡
- 손목 ------------------- ⬡
- 발목 ------------------- ⬡
- 근육 ------------------- ⬡
- 예방하다 ------------- ⬡
- 스트레칭 ------------- ⬡
- 적어도 ---------------- ⬡
- 안전하다 ------------- ⬡

Day 33

Let's warm up!

Imagine the situation in the story below to
remember the ten Korean words in context.

체력을 **관리하기** 위해서 운동을 시작했다.

To **manage** my **physical fitness**, I started exercising.

한동안 운동을 안 하다가 하니까 **손목**과 **발목**이
아팠다.

I had not exercised **in a while**, so my **wrist** and **ankle** hurt.

병원에 가니까 **근육**을 다쳤다고 했다.

I went to the hospital, and the doctor said that I hurt my **muscles**.

다치는 것을 **예방하려면** 운동하기 전에 **스트레칭**
을 해야 한다.

To **prevent** injury, I have to **stretch** before exercising.

앞으로 **적어도** 10분은 스트레칭을 해서 **안전하게**
운동할 것이다.

From now on, I will stretch for **at least** 10 minutes and exercise
safely.

Let's keep the ball rolling!

Word	Meaning	Example
체력	physical strength[fitness]	체력이 너무 약해서 고민이에요. My physical strength is too weak, so I'm worried about it.
관리하다	to manage, to take care of	건강은 젊을 때부터 관리해야 돼요. You have to take care of your health from an early age.
한동안	for a while, in a while	한동안 매운 음식을 못 먹었어요. I couldn't eat spicy food for a while.
손목	wrist	테니스 치다가 오른쪽 손목을 다쳤어요. While I was playing tennis, I hurt my right wrist.
발목	ankle	발목까지 오는 코트를 찾고 있어요. I'm looking for an ankle-length coat.
근육	muscle	요새 운동을 열심히 해서 팔에 근육이 생겼어요. Lately I exercised hard, so I gained muscles in my arm.

예방하다	to prevent	감기를 예방하려면 손을 자주 씻어야 돼요. To prevent catching a cold, you have to wash your hands often.
스트레칭	stretch	저는 아침에 일어나자마자 스트레칭을 해요. As soon as I wake up in the morning, I do some stretches.
적어도	at least	일주일에 적어도 세 번은 운동을 해야 돼요. You have to exercise at least three times a week.
안전하다	to be safe	아이들이 안전하게 놀 수 있는 공간이 필요해요. We need a safe place for children to play.

Let's review!

Complete the story from Day 33 using the words you just learned.

_____을 _____ 위해서 운동을 시작했다.

_____ 운동을 안 하다가 하니까 _____과 _____이 아팠다.

병원에 가니까 _____을 다쳤다고 했다.

다치는 것을 _____ 운동하기 전에 _____을
해야 한다.

앞으로 _____ 10분은 스트레칭을 해서 _____ 운동할
것이다.

Translation

To **manage** my **physical fitness**, I started exercising. I had not exercised **in a while**, so my **wrist** and **ankle** hurt. I went to the hospital, and the doctor said that I hurt my **muscles**. To **prevent** injury, I have to **stretch** before exercising. From now on, I will stretch for **at least** 10 minutes and exercise **safely**.

Word Search - Find 7 words out of the vocabulary you just learned in this chapter.

석	체	력	암	마	손	넘
경	략	작	야	더	목	서
스	트	레	칭	대	효	적
진	인	다	호	발	애	어
서	트	레	쓰	목	서	도
한	동	안	연	혜	근	록
윤	수	냐	욱	용	육	숭

Fill in the blanks with Korean words that matches its English translation.

Word bank	
체력	근육
관리하다	예방하다
한동안	스트레칭
손목	적어도
발목	안전하다

01 to manage, to take care of

_____

02 stretch

_____

03 to prevent

_____

04 to be safe

_____

05 muscle

_____

Day 34

⬡ **월드컵** ------------------ ⬡

⬡ **경기** ------------------ ⬡

⬡ **입국하다** ------------------ ⬡

⬡ **추천** ------------------ ⬡

⬡ **행사** ------------------ ⬡

⬡ **통역** ------------------ ⬡

⬡ **감독** ------------------ ⬡

⬡ **사인** ------------------ ⬡

⬡ **경험** ------------------ ⬡

⬡ **올림픽** ------------------ ⬡

....

Imagine the situation in the story below to remember the ten Korean words in context.

전 세계의 선수들이 월드컵 경기를 위해서 우리나라에 입국했다.

Players from all over the world <u>entered</u> Korea for <u>the World Cup games</u>.

나는 교수님의 추천으로 월드컵 행사에서 통역을 하게 되었다.

I got to <u>interpret</u> at the World Cup <u>event</u> because of a <u>recommendation</u> from my professor.

유명한 축구 감독과 선수들을 만나서 사인을 받았다.

I met famous soccer <u>coaches</u> and players, and I got their <u>autographs</u>.

아주 좋은 경험이었다.

It was a very good <u>experience</u>.

2년 후 올림픽 행사에서도 내가 통역을 하고 싶다.

I would like to interpret at <u>the Olympic Games</u> event coming in two years.

Let's keep the ball rolling!

Word	Meaning	Example
월드컵	the World Cup	이번 월드컵에서 어느 나라가 우승할 것 같아요? Which country do you think will win this World Cup?
경기	game, match	한국과 브라질의 축구 경기가 오늘 밤 8시에 있어요. There's a soccer match between Korea and Brazil tonight at 8 p.m.
입국하다	to enter (a country)	캐나다 입국할 때 비자 필요해요? Do I need a visa to enter Canada?
추천	recommendation	대학원에 입학하려면 교수님 추천이 필요해요. To enter graduate school, you need a recommendation from a professor.
행사	event	비가 와서 행사가 취소됐어요. Because of the rain, the event has been canceled.
통역	interpretation	영어를 잘해서 통역이 필요 없어요. I speak English well, so I don't need interpretation.

감독	coach, manager	곧 새로운 감독님이 온다고 들었어요. I heard that a new coach is coming soon.
사인	autograph	벽에 연예인 사인이 많이 붙어 있네요. There are a lot of celebrity autographs on the walls.
경험	experience	다양한 경험을 더 많이 해 보고 싶어요. I want to have more diverse experiences.
올림픽	the Olympic Games	올림픽에 나가는 게 꿈이에요. It's my dream to take part in the Olympic Games.

Let's review!

Complete the story from Day 34 using the words you just learned.

전 세계의 선수들이 _____ _____를 위해서 우리나라에

_____.

나는 교수님의 _____으로 월드컵 _____에서 _____을 하게 되
었다.

유명한 축구 _____과 선수들을 만나서 _____을 받았다.

아주 좋은 _____이었다.

2년 후 _____ 행사에서도 내가 통역을 하고 싶다.

....

Translation

Players from all over the world <u>entered</u> Korea for <u>the World Cup</u> <u>games</u>. I got to <u>interpret</u> at the World Cup <u>event</u> because of a <u>recommendation</u> from my professor. I met famous soccer <u>coaches</u> and players, and I got their <u>autographs</u>. It was a very good <u>experience</u>. I would like to interpret at <u>the Olympic Games</u> event coming in two years.

Crossword Puzzle

01 game, match

02 event

03 the Olympic Games

04 the World Cup

05 experience

06 autograph

07 interpretation

Fill in the blanks with Korean words that matches its English translation.

Word bank	
월드컵	통역
경기	감독
입국하다	사인
추천	경험
행사	올림픽

01 to enter (a country) _____

02 interpretation _____

03 recommendation _____

04 game, match _____

05 coach, manager _____

Day 35

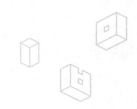

- 학기 -------------------- ○
- 주변 -------------------- ○
- 원룸 -------------------- ○
- 월세 -------------------- ○
- 계약 -------------------- ○
- 전세 -------------------- ○
- 통장 -------------------- ○
- 확인하다 ---------------- ○
- 저축하다 ---------------- ○
- 매달 -------------------- ○

Day 35

Let's warm up!

Imagine the situation in the story below to remember the ten Korean words in context.

다음 **학기**부터 학교 **주변 원룸**에 살고 싶다.

I want to live in a <u>studio apartment</u> <u>near</u> my school starting next <u>semester</u>.

월세 계약이 좋을까, **전세** 계약이 좋을까?

Which one is better, a <u>monthly lease</u> <u>contract</u> or a <u>Jeonse</u> contract?

통장을 **확인해** 보니까 **저축한** 돈이 별로 없다.

I <u>checked</u> my <u>bankbook</u>, and I see that I do not have much money <u>saved</u>.

전세 계약을 하려면 많은 돈이 필요하다.

I need a lot of money to make a Jeonse contract.

매달 돈을 내는 것이 싫지만, 월세로 계약을 해야 될 것 같다.

I hate to pay <u>monthly</u>, but I think I will have to make a monthly lease contract.

Let's keep the ball rolling!

Word	Meaning	Example
학기	semester	이번 학기에 다섯 과목을 들어야 돼요. I have to take five classes this semester.
주변	surroundings, vicinity	공원 주변에는 주차할 곳이 없어요. There's no parking space in the vicinity of the park.
원룸	studio apartment	원룸에 살고 있어요. I'm living in a studio apartment.
월세	monthly lease	월세가 너무 비싸서 다른 집을 알아보려고 해요. The monthly lease is too expensive, so I'm looking for another house.
계약	contract	이번 달에 계약이 끝나요. The contract ends this month.

전세	Jeonse (Korea's unique rental system with a long-term and substantial deposit)	전세 제도는 한국에만 있어요. The Jeonse system only exists in Korea.
통장	bankbook	은행 갈 때 통장 가지고 가세요. When you go to the bank, take your bankbook with you.
확인하다	to check	여행 날짜를 다시 확인해 보세요. Please check your travel dates again.
저축하다	to save	한 달에 얼마씩 저축해? How much money do you save per month?
매달	every[each] month, monthly	저는 부모님에게 매달 용돈을 드려요. I give my parents allowance every month.

Let's review!

Complete the story from Day 35 using the words you just learned.

다음 _____부터 학교 _____ _____에 살고 싶다.

_____ _____이 좋을까, _____ 계약이 좋을까?

_____을 _____ 보니까 _____ 돈이 별로 없다.

전세 계약을 하려면 많은 돈이 필요하다.

_____ 돈을 내는 것이 싫지만, 월세로 계약을 해야 될 것 같다.

Translation

I want to live in a <u>studio apartment</u> <u>near</u> my school starting next <u>semester</u>. Which one is better, a <u>monthly lease</u> <u>contract</u> or a <u>Jeonse</u> contract? I <u>checked</u> my <u>bankbook</u>, and I see that I do not have much money <u>saved</u>. I need a lot of money to make a Jeonse contract. I hate to pay <u>monthly</u>, but I think I will have to make a monthly lease contract.

Word Search – Find 7 words out of the vocabulary you just learned in this chapter.

알	기	희	원	룸	율	잔
학	구	완	세	윤	광	세
기	연	텅	장	태	소	시
영	전	훈	예	계	약	지
월	세	누	라	역	보	모
래	사	승	확	인	하	다
매	달	수	언	효	진	은

....

Fill in the blanks with Korean words that matches its English translation.

Word bank	
학기	전세
주변	통장
원룸	확인하다
월세	저축하다
계약	매달

01 to save   _____

02 to check   _____

03 contract   _____

04 surroundings, vicinity   _____

05 bankbook   _____

Day 36

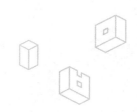

⬡ **전하다** ----------------- ◯

⬡ **전국적** ----------------- ◯

⬡ **햇볕** ----------------- ◯

⬡ **강하다** ----------------- ◯

⬡ **기온** ----------------- ◯

⬡ **떨어지다** ----------------- ◯

⬡ **예정** ----------------- ◯

⬡ **외출하다** ----------------- ◯

⬡ **외투** ----------------- ◯

⬡ **챙기다** ----------------- ◯

Day 36

Imagine the situation in the story below to
remember the ten Korean words in context.

날씨 뉴스를 **전해** 드리겠습니다.

I will <u>deliver</u> the weather news to you.

오늘 낮에는 **전국적**으로 **햇볕**이 뜨겁고 **강하겠습
니다**.

Today, the <u>sun</u> will be hot and <u>strong</u> during the day throughout
<u>the whole country</u>.

하지만 밤에는 **기온**이 많이 **떨어질 예정**인데요.

However, the <u>temperatures</u> are <u>expected</u> to <u>drop</u> a lot at night.

밤부터 비가 오는 곳도 있겠습니다.

There will be places where it starts raining at night.

외출하실 때 우산과 **외투**를 꼭 **챙기시길**
바랍니다.

When you <u>go out</u>, be sure to <u>bring</u> an umbrella and a <u>coat</u>.

Let's keep the ball rolling!

Word	Meaning	Example
전하다	to deliver, to tell	걱정하지 말라고 전해 주세요. Please tell them not to worry.
전국적	the whole country	내일 전국적으로 많은 비가 내릴 것으로 보입니다. It looks like it'll rain heavily throughout the whole country tomorrow.
햇볕	sunlight, sun	햇볕이 너무 따뜻해서 졸려요. I'm sleepy because the sun is so warm.
강하다	to be strong	내일까지 바람이 강하게 분다고 합니다. It's said that the wind will blow strongly until tomorrow.
기온	temperature	다음 주부터 기온이 다시 올라간다고 해요. Temperatures are expected to rise again from next week.
떨어지다	to drop	학교 성적이 떨어져서 걱정이에요. I'm worried about my low school grades.

예정	expectation, anticipation	회의가 예정보다 일찍 끝날 것 같아요. I think the meeting will end earlier than scheduled.
외출하다	to go out	외출하기 전에 선크림 꼭 발라요. Before going out, make sure to put on sunblock.
외투	coat	외투는 여기 놔두면 돼요. You can leave your coat here.
챙기다	to bring	제 가방도 좀 챙겨 주세요. Please bring my bag, too.

Let's review!

Complete the story from Day 36 using the words you just learned.

날씨 뉴스를 _____ 드리겠습니다.

오늘 낮에는 _____으로 _____이 뜨겁고 _____.

하지만 밤에는 _____이 많이 _____ _____인데요.

밤부터 비가 오는 곳도 있겠습니다.

_____ 때 우산과 _____를 꼭 _____ 바랍니다.

Translation

I will <u>deliver</u> the weather news to you. Today, the <u>sun</u> will be hot and <u>strong</u> during the day throughout <u>the whole country</u>. However, the <u>temperatures</u> are <u>expected</u> to <u>drop</u> a lot at night. There will be places where it starts raining at night. When you <u>go out</u>, be sure to <u>bring</u> an umbrella and a <u>coat</u>.

Crossword Puzzle

01					02	
		03				
				04		
05						
		06				
07						

01   sunlight, sun

02   coat

03   to drop

04   to bring

05   to be strong

06   temperature

07   expectation, anticipation

Fill in the blanks with Korean words that matches its English translation.

Word bank	
전하다 전국적 햇볕 강하다 기온	떨어지다 예정 외출하다 외투 챙기다

01   the whole country   _____

02   to bring   _____

03   to deliver, to tell   _____

04   to go out   _____

05   sunlight, sun   _____

Day 37

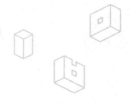

- 원피스 ----------------- ○
- 분명히 ---------------- ○
- 허락 ------------------ ○
- 없이 ------------------ ○
- 만지다 ---------------- ○
- 막 -------------------- ○
- 끊다 ------------------ ○
- 옷장 ------------------ ○
- 바닥 ------------------ ○
- 후회하다 -------------- ○

Day 37

Let's warm up!

....

*Imagine the situation in the story below to
remember the ten Korean words in context.*

내가 정말 좋아하는 원피스가 사라졌다.

The <u>dress</u> that I really like has disappeared.

나는 분명히 언니가 입고 나갔을 거라고 생각했다.

I <u>definitely</u> thought that my older sister wore it and went out.

언니는 항상 내 물건을 허락 없이 만진다.

My older sister always <u>touches</u> my things <u>without</u> my <u>permission</u>.

나는 언니한테 전화해서 막 화를 냈다.

I called my older sister, and <u>harshly</u> went off on her.

**그런데 전화를 끊고 보니까 옷장 바닥에 원피스가
있었다.**

But after I <u>hung up</u> the phone, I found the dress on the <u>floor</u> of
the <u>closet</u>.

나는 언니에게 화낸 것을 후회했다.

I <u>regretted</u> that I got angry at my older sister.

Let's keep the ball rolling!

Word	Meaning	Example
원피스	dress	경은 씨가 원피스 입은 거 처음 봐요. It's the first time that I've seen Kyeong-eun wearing a dress.
분명히	clearly, definitely	내일은 분명히 비가 올 거예요. It'll definitely rain tomorrow.
허락	permission	여행 가려면 엄마 허락이 필요해요. I need my mom's permission to go on a trip.
없이	without	핸드폰 없이 일주일 살기에 도전해 봤어요. I tried challenging myself to live a week without my cell phone.
만지다	to touch	내 머리 좀 만지지 마. Please don't touch my hair.
막	severely, harshly, really	이 콘서트에서는 소리를 막 질러도 괜찮아요. It's okay to scream really loudly at this concert.

끊다	to hang up	우리 "하나, 둘, 셋" 하면 동시에 전화 끊자. When we say "one, two, three", let's hang up the phone at the same time.
옷장	closet	옷장을 정리하다가 잃어버린 양말을 발견했어요. While cleaning out my closet, I found my missing socks.
바닥	floor	바닥에 떨어진 음식은 3초 안에만 주우면 괜찮아요. It's okay to pick up food that fell on the floor if it's within three seconds.
후회하다	to regret	대학생 때 공부만 한 게 후회돼요. I regret that I did nothing but study when I was in university.

Let's review!

Complete the story from Day 37 using the words you just learned.

내가 정말 좋아하는 _____가 사라졌다.

나는 _____ 언니가 입고 나갔을 거라고 생각했다.

언니는 항상 내 물건을 ____ ____ _____.

나는 언니한테 전화해서 ___ 화를 냈다.

그런데 전화를 _____ 보니까 _____ _____에 원피스가 있었다.

나는 언니에게 화낸 것을 _____.

Translation

The **dress** that I really like has disappeared. I **definitely** thought that my older sister wore it and went out. My older sister always **touches** my things **without** my **permission**. I called my older sister, and **harshly** went off on her. But after I **hung up** the phone, I found the dress on the **floor** of the **closet**. I **regretted** that I got angry at my older sister.

Word Search – Find 7 words out of the vocabulary you just learned in this chapter.

하	김	니	분	명	히	정
락	원	막	선	빼	엘	바
헤	피	선	없	이	옷	닥
진	스	우	먹	빈	효	통
윤	다	니	재	아	만	현
사	호	후	하	다	지	영
옷	장	욱	용	끊	다	규

....

Fill in the blanks with Korean words that matches its English translation.

Word bank	
원피스	막
분명히	끊다
허락	옷장
없이	바닥
만지다	후회하다

01 severely, harshly, really

_____

02 to touch

_____

03 permission

_____

04 without

_____

05 to regret

_____

Day 38

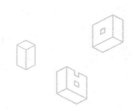

- 사업가 ------------------ ○
- 관찰하다 ----------------- ○
- 아이디어 ----------------- ○
- 떠오르다 ----------------- ○
- 연구하다 ----------------- ○
- 실제 -------------------- ○
- 일상생활 ----------------- ○
- 기계 -------------------- ○
- 발명하다 ----------------- ○
- 부자 -------------------- ○

Let's warm up!

....

Imagine the situation in the story below to remember the ten Korean words in context.

나는 **사업가**다.

I am a <u>business person</u>.

나는 주변을 **관찰하는** 걸 좋아한다.

I like to <u>observe</u> my surroundings.

그러다가 재미있는 **아이디어**가 **떠오를** 때가 있다.

And then there are times when an interesting <u>idea</u> <u>comes to my mind</u>.

나는 조금 더 **연구해서** 이 아이디어로 **실제** 제품을 만든다.

I <u>research</u> some more, and make an <u>actual</u> product with this idea.

이렇게 해서 나는 **일상생활**에서 사용할 수 있는 여러 가지 **기계**를 **발명했다**.

In this way, I have <u>invented</u> several <u>gadgets</u> that can be used in <u>daily life</u>.

이 기계들 덕분에 나는 **부자**가 될 수 있었다.

Thanks to these machines, I was able to become a <u>rich person</u>.

Let's keep the ball rolling!

Word	Meaning	Example
사업가	business person	와이셔츠 입으니까 성공한 사업가 같아요. Wearing a dress shirt, you look like a successful business person.
관찰하다	to observe	지하철이나 버스를 탈 때 사람들을 관찰하는 걸 좋아해요. When I'm on the subway or bus, I like observing people.
아이디어	idea	좋은 아이디어 있으면 말해 주세요. Let me know if you have any good ideas.
떠오르다	to strike, to come to one's mind	방금 재미있는 생각이 떠올랐어요. An interesting thought just came to my mind.
연구하다	to research, to study	대학에서 우주를 연구하고 있어요. I'm studying the universe at university.
실제	actuality, reality	지금 이거 실제 상황 맞아요? Is this a real situation in reality now?

일상생활	everyday[daily] life	한국인들이 일상생활에서 가장 많이 사용하는 표현을 알려 줄게요. I'll teach you the expressions that Koreans use the most in their daily lives.
기계	machine, gadget	제가 만지기만 하면 기계가 망가져요. Whenever I handle a machine, it breaks down.
발명하다	to invent	텔레비전을 발명한 사람이 누군지 알아요? Do you know who invented the television?
부자	rich person	만약에 부자가 되면 뭘 하고 싶어요? What would you like to do if you could become a rich person?

Let's review!

Complete the story from Day 38 using the words you just learned.

나는 _____다.

나는 주변을 _____ 걸 좋아한다.

그러다가 재미있는 _____가 _____ 때가 있다.

나는 조금 더 _____ 이 아이디어로 _____ 제품을 만든다.

이렇게 해서 나는 _____에서 사용할 수 있는 여러 가지 _____를 _____.

이 기계들 덕분에 나는 _____가 될 수 있었다.

Translation

I am a **business person**. I like to **observe** my surroundings. And then there are times when an interesting **idea comes to my mind**. I **research** some more, and make an **actual** product with this idea. In this way, I have **invented** several **gadgets** that can be used in **daily life**. Thanks to these machines, I was able to become a **rich person**.

Crossword Puzzle

01 business person
02 machine, gadget
03 rich person
04 everyday[daily] life
05 actuality, reality
06 idea
07 to observe

Fill in the blanks with Korean words that matches its English translation.

Word bank	
사업가	실제
관찰하다	일상생활
아이디어	기계
떠오르다	발명하다
연구하다	부자

01 to strike, to come to one's mind _____

02 actuality, reality _____

03 to research, to study _____

04 to invent _____

05 to observe _____

Day 39

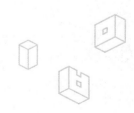

◆ **지역** ------------------------ ◯

◆ **고객** ------------------------ ◯

◆ **질** ---------------------------- ◯

◆ **재료** ------------------------ ◯

◆ **기르다** --------------------- ◯

◆ **특징** ------------------------ ◯

◆ **쌀** ---------------------------- ◯

◆ **양념** ------------------------ ◯

◆ **인스턴트** ------------------ ◯

◆ **입맛** ------------------------ ◯

Day 39

Let's warm up!

....

Imagine the situation in the story below to remember the ten Korean words in context.

이 **지역**에는 유명한 식당이 있다.

There is a famous restaurant in this <u>area</u>.

이 식당은 언제나 **고객**을 위해 **질** 좋은 **재료**를 준비한다.

This restaurant always prepares high <u>quality</u> <u>ingredients</u> for their <u>customers</u>.

재료로 쓸 채소를 직접 **기르는** 것이 이 식당의 **특징**이다.

The <u>special characteristic</u> of this restaurant is that they <u>grow</u> their vegetables themselves to use as ingredients in their dishes.

직접 기른 채소와 **쌀**로 요리를 한다.

They cook with the vegetables and <u>rice</u> that they grew themselves.

그리고 **양념**까지 직접 만든다.

And they even make their own <u>sauce</u>.

인스턴트를 좋아하는 사람도, **입맛**이 없는 사람도 이 식당에 오면 밥을 다 잘 먹는다.

Even people who like <u>instant foods</u> and people who have no <u>appetite</u> can eat well when they come to this restaurant.

Let's keep the ball rolling!

Word	Meaning	Example
지역	area	이 지역에서 가장 유명한 게 뭐예요? What's the most famous thing in this area?
고객	customer	젊은 고객에게 인기가 많은 제품이에요. This product is popular with young customers.
질	quality	저는 질보다 양이 더 중요해요. For me, quantity is more important than quality.
재료	ingredient, material	재료는 제가 다 준비해 놓았어요. I've prepared all the ingredients.
기르다	to grow, to raise	아이들이 직접 기른 채소예요. These are the vegetables that the children grew themselves.
특징	feature, characteristic	한국인의 특징을 말해 보세요. Tell me about the characteristics of Koreans.

쌀	rice	**쌀로 만든 아이스크림 먹어 봤어요?**
		Have you ever tried ice cream made with rice?
양념	seasoning, sauce	**양념 맛이 너무 강해서 별로예요.**
		The flavor of the seasoning is too strong so I don't like it.
인스턴트	instant (food)	**인스턴트에 너무 익숙해지면 안 돼요.**
		Don't get too used to instant foods.
입맛	appetite, one's palate	**입맛이 없어서 밥을 못 먹겠어요.**
		I have no appetite, so I can't eat.

Let's review!

Complete the story from Day 39 using the words you just learned.

이 _____에는 유명한 식당이 있다.

이 식당은 언제나 _____을 위해 ___ 좋은 _____를 준비한다.

재료로 쓸 채소를 직접 _____ 것이 이 식당의 _____이다.

직접 기른 채소와 ___로 요리를 한다.

그리고 _____까지 직접 만든다.

_____를 좋아하는 사람도, _____이 없는 사람도 이 식당에 오면 밥을 다 잘 먹는다.

Translation

There is a famous restaurant in this <u>area</u>. This restaurant always prepares high <u>quality</u> <u>ingredients</u> for their <u>customers</u>. The <u>special characteristic</u> of this restaurant is that they <u>grow</u> their vegetables themselves to use as ingredients in their dishes. They cook with the vegetables and <u>rice</u> that they grew themselves. And they even make their own <u>sauce</u>. Even people who like <u>instant foods</u> and people who have no <u>appetite</u> can eat well when they come to this restaurant.

Word Search – Find 7 words out of the vocabulary you just learned in this chapter.

양	념	져	고	갱	특	징
최	영	텍	객	조	스	턱
입	맛	하	귀	좌	인	음
효	턱	랩	카	요	스	봅
멋	재	폰	마	학	턴	방
네	료	예	세	성	트	현
이	다	기	르	다	훈	박

....

Fill in the blanks with Korean words that matches its English translation.

Word bank	
지역	특징
고객	쌀
질	양념
재료	인스턴트
기르다	입맛

01 appetite, one's palate   _____

02 area   _____

03 quality   _____

04 ingredient, material   _____

05 rice   _____

Day 40

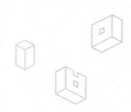

- **천장** --------------- ⬡
- **대형** --------------- ⬡
- **달다** --------------- ⬡
- **설명서** ------------- ⬡
- **냉방** --------------- ⬡
- **난방** --------------- ⬡
- **틀다** --------------- ⬡
- **고생하다** ----------- ⬡
- **서비스** ------------- ⬡
- **문의하다** ----------- ⬡

Day 40

Let's warm up!

....

Imagine the situation in the story below to remember the ten Korean words in context.

회사 **천장**에 **대형** 에어컨을 **달았다**.

We **installed** a **large** air conditioner on the **ceiling** of the office.

설명서에는 **냉방**과 **난방** 기능이 모두 되는 에어컨이라고 쓰여 있었다.

In the **instruction manual**, it was written that it was an air conditioner with both **cooling** and **heating** functions.

그런데 에어컨을 **틀어** 보니까 따뜻한 바람이 나오지 않았다.

However, when we **turned on** the air conditioner, there was no warm air coming out.

겨울에 **고생할** 것 같아서 **서비스** 센터에 **문의**했다.

We thought we would **have trouble** in the winter, so we **asked** the **service** center about it.

다행히 서비스 센터에서 에어컨을 고쳐 줬다.

Fortunately, the service center fixed the air conditioner.

Let's keep the ball rolling!

Word	Meaning	Example
천장	ceiling	모기가 천장에 붙어 있어요. A mosquito is sitting on the ceiling.
대형	large size	사무실에 사람들이 많아져서 대형 냉장고를 사야 할 것 같아요. There are many people in the office now, so I think we should buy a large refrigerator.
달다	to install	선풍기 어디에 달까요? Where should I install the fan?
설명서	instruction manual	설명서를 꼼꼼히 읽어 보세요. Read the manual carefully.
냉방	cooling, air-conditioning	냉방이 너무 세서 추워요. The air-conditioning is too strong, so it's cold.
난방	heating	여기 난방 잘되고 있는 거 맞아요? Are you sure that the heating is working well here?

| **틀다** | to turn on | 어젯밤에 너무 더워서 선풍기 틀고 잤어요. |
| | | It was very hot last night, so I slept with the fan on. |

| **고생하다** | to have a hard time, to have trouble | 일하는 동안 너무 고생한 것 같아서 미안해요. |
| | | I'm sorry that you had a hard time while working. |

| **서비스** | service | 노트북이 고장 나서 서비스 센터에 가 보려고요. |
| | | My laptop is broken and I'm thinking of going to the service center. |

| **문의하다** | to ask, to inquire | 회사에 문의했는데, 아직 답변이 안 왔어요. |
| | | I asked the company, but I haven't received a reply yet. |

Let's review!

Complete the story from Day 40 using the words you just learned.

회사 _____에 _____ 에어컨을 _____.

_____에는 _____과 _____ 기능이 모두 되는 에어컨이라고 쓰여 있었다.

그런데 에어컨을 _____ 보니까 따뜻한 바람이 나오지 않았다.

겨울에 _____ 것 같아서 _____ 센터에 _____.

다행히 서비스 센터에서 에어컨을 고쳐 줬다.

Translation

We <u>installed</u> a <u>large</u> air conditioner on the <u>ceiling</u> of the office. In the <u>instruction manual</u>, it was written that it was an air conditioner with both <u>cooling</u> and <u>heating</u> functions. However, when we <u>turned on</u> the air conditioner, there was no warm air coming out. We thought we would <u>have trouble</u> in the winter, so we <u>asked</u> the <u>service</u> center about it. Fortunately, the service center fixed the air conditioner.

Crossword Puzzle

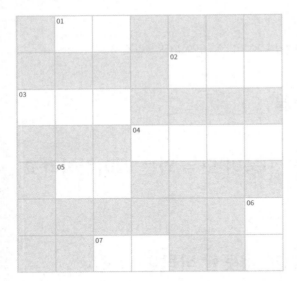

01 large size

02 instruction manual

03 service

04 to ask, to inquire

05 ceiling

06 heating

07 to install

Fill in the blanks with Korean words that matches its English translation.

Word bank	
천장	난방
대형	틀다
달다	고생하다
설명서	서비스
냉방	문의하다

01 cooling, air-conditioning _____

02 to install _____

03 instruction manual _____

04 to turn on _____

05 to have a hard time, to have trouble _____

01 Choose the word that is <u>inedible</u>.
   a. 설명서   **b.** 인스턴트   **c.** 삼겹살   **d.** 김치찌개

02 Choose the word that is <u>not</u> a job.
   a. 사업가   **b.** 부자   **c.** 감독   **d.** 선수

03 Choose the best place to put 외투.
   a. 천장   **b.** 주변   **c.** 옷장   **d.** 지역

04 What is the Korean word for the item in the picture? _____

05 Which of the following words does <u>not</u> belong as a 재료?
   a. 양념   **b.** 쌀   **c.** 된장   **d.** 입맛

06 Choose the word that is <u>not</u> related to emotions.

    a. 귀찮다   b. 후회하다   c. 기쁘다   d. 떨어지다

07 Choose the word that best fits in the blank.

> 일주일에 _____ 세 번은 운동을 해야 돼요.
> = You have to exercise at least three times a week.

    a. 적어도   b. 적으면   c. 많아도   d. 많으면

08 Choose the pair of antonyms that are matched correctly.

    a. 전세 - 월세   b. 체력 - 근육
    c. 냉방 - 난방   d. 끊다 - 달다

09 Choose one that you can touch.

    a. 계약   b. 허락   c. 경험   d. 기계

10 Which of the following has the longest interval?

    a. 매주   b. 매달   c. 매우   d. 매일

[11-20] Fill in the blanks using the words that you learned in Day 31 - Day 40.

11 넘어져서 무릎에 _____이/가 생겼어요.
    = I fell down, so I got a bruise on my knee.

12 너무 창피해서 _____ 싶었어요.
    = I was so embarrassed that I wanted to hide.

13 건강은 젊을 때부터 _____ 돼요.
    = You have to take care of your health from an early age.

14 캐나다 _____ 때 비자 필요해요?
    = Do I need a visa to enter Canada?

15 이번 _____에 다섯 과목을 들어야 돼요.
    = I have to take five classes this semester.

16 내일까지 바람이 _____ 분다고 합니다.
    = It's said that the wind will blow strongly until tomorrow.

17 핸드폰 _____ 일주일 살기에 도전해 봤어요.

= I tried challenging myself to live a week without my cell phone.

18 대학에서 우주를 _____ 있어요.

= I'm studying the universe at university.

19 젊은 _____에게 인기가 많은 제품이에요.

= This product is popular with young customers.

20 일하는 동안 너무 _____ 것 같아서 미안해요.

= I'm sorry that you had a hard time while working.

Day 41

⬡ 해수욕장 ----------------- ◯

⬡ 모래 -------------------- ◯

⬡ 눈부시다 --------------- ◯

⬡ 싱싱하다 --------------- ◯

⬡ 저렴하다 --------------- ◯

⬡ 새우 -------------------- ◯

⬡ 환하다 ----------------- ◯

⬡ 공기 -------------------- ◯

⬡ 먼지 -------------------- ◯

⬡ 실컷 -------------------- ◯

Day 41

Imagine the situation in the story below to remember the ten Korean words in context.

해수욕장에 갔다.

I went to the <u>beach</u>.

수영도 하고 모래도 가지고 놀았다.

I swam and played with <u>sand</u>.

날씨가 좋아서 햇빛이 눈부셨다.

The weather was nice, so the sun was <u>dazzling</u>.

오후에는 시장에 갔다.

I went to a market in the afternoon.

싱싱한 해산물을 저렴하게 먹을 수 있어서 좋았다.

It was nice that we could eat <u>fresh</u> seafood at a <u>cheap</u> price.

특히 새우가 정말 맛있었다.

Especially, the <u>shrimp</u> was really delicious.

밤에 별도 환하게 잘 보였다.

The stars were <u>brightly</u> visible at night.

공기가 좋아서 먼지가 없는 것 같았다.

The <u>air</u> was good, so there seemed to be no <u>dust</u>.

하루 종일 실컷 놀아서 잠이 잘 왔다.

I had <u>so much</u> fun all day, so I slept well.

Let's keep the ball rolling!

Word	Meaning	Example
해수욕장	beach	이번 여름에 해수욕장에 한 번도 못 갔어요. I didn't go to the beach even once this summer.
모래	sand	신발에 모래가 들어갔어요. There's sand in my shoes.
눈부시다	to be too bright, to dazzle one's eyes	햇빛이 너무 눈부셔서 눈을 못 뜨겠어요. The sun is too dazzling, so I can't open my eyes.
싱싱하다	to be fresh	재료들이 다 싱싱해서 너무 맛있어요. The ingredients are all fresh, so it's really delicious.
저렴하다	to be cheap	생각보다 가격이 저렴해서 놀랐어요. The price was cheaper than I thought, so I was surprised.
새우	shrimp	저는 잘 때 새우처럼 허리를 구부리고 자요. When I sleep, I crouch my back like a shrimp.

환하다	to be bright	8시인데도 밖이 환해요. Even at 8 o'clock, it's bright outside.
공기	air	오늘 공기가 너무 안 좋아요. The air is so bad today.
먼지	dust	와, 텔레비전 위에 쌓인 먼지 좀 봐요. Wow, look at the dust on the television.
실컷	heartily, as much as one likes[wishes]	이번 주말에는 실컷 먹고 자려고요. This weekend, I'm going to eat and sleep as much as I want.

Let's review!

Complete the story from Day 41 using the words you just learned.

_____에 갔다.

수영도 하고 _____도 가지고 놀았다.

날씨가 좋아서 햇빛이 _____.

오후에는 시장에 갔다.

_____ 해산물을 _____ 먹을 수 있어서 좋았다.

특히 _____가 정말 맛있었다.

밤에 별도 _____ 잘 보였다.

_____가 좋아서 _____가 없는 것 같았다.

하루 종일 _____ 놀아서 잠이 잘 왔다.

Translation

I went to the **beach**. I swam and played with **sand**. The weather was nice, so the sun was **dazzling**. I went to a market in the afternoon. It was nice that we could eat **fresh** seafood at a **cheap** price. Especially, the **shrimp** was really delicious. The stars were **brightly** visible at night. The **air** was good, so there seemed to be no **dust**. I had **so much** fun all day, so I slept well.

Word Search - Find 7 words out of the vocabulary you just learned in this chapter.

지	먼	해	수	욕	장	호
실	컷	코	세	우	훤	연
준	화	다	영	환	하	다
모	경	순	싱	선	자	요
래	마	범	싱	재	렴	아
수	존	성	하	혜	공	호
눈	부	시	다	숙	기	강

Fill in the blanks with Korean words that matches its English translation.

Word bank	
해수욕장	새우
모래	환하다
눈부시다	공기
싱싱하다	먼지
저렴하다	실컷

01 to be fresh _____

02 to be cheap _____

03 dust _____

04 shrimp _____

05 air _____

Day 42

Day 42

Imagine the situation in the story below to
remember the ten Korean words in context.

내 **사촌** 동생은 **통통하다**.

My younger <u>cousin</u> is <u>plump</u>.

내가 보기에는 귀여운데, 동생은 **본인**이 너무 **살쪘
다고** 생각한다.

He looks cute to me, but he thinks <u>he</u> is too <u>fat</u>.

그래서 요즘 살을 **빼려고** 밥을 **굶는다고** 한다.

So he says that he <u>skips meals</u> to <u>lose</u> weight these days.

마음은 **이해하지만**, 굶는 것은 몸에 안 좋다.

I <u>understand</u> how he feels, but skipping meals is bad for the body.

그래서 나는 동생에게 **꾸준히** 운동을 하라고 말했다.

So I told him to exercise <u>steadily</u>.

그리고 **헬스장 비용**을 대신 내 주었다.

And I paid for his <u>gym</u> membership <u>fees</u>.

사촌 동생은 이제 꾸준히 운동을 한다.

My younger cousin works out steadily now.

Let's keep the ball rolling!

Word	Meaning	Example
사촌	cousin	저는 사촌이랑 별로 안 친해요. I'm not very close with my cousin.
통통하다	to be plump, to be chubby	저는 어렸을 때 키가 작고 통통했어요. I was short and chubby when I was young.
본인	oneself	본인이 와서 서류를 작성해야 돼요. You must come yourself and complete the document.
살찌다	to gain weight	요즘 너무 살쪄서 좀 적게 먹으려고 해요. I've been gaining a lot of weight lately, so I'm trying to eat less.
빼다	to lose (weight)	살찌는 건 쉬운데, 빼는 건 너무 어려워요. Gaining weight is easy, but losing weight is very hard.
굶다	to skip[miss] a meal, to starve	어제 저녁부터 굶어서 너무 배가 고파요. I haven't eaten since last night, so I'm very hungry.

이해하다	to understand	**이해해 줘서 고마워.** Thank you for your understanding.
꾸준히	steadily, consistently, persistently	**조금씩이라도 꾸준히 하는 게 제일 중요해요.** It's most important to do it consistently, even a little at a time.
헬스장	gym	**저는 매일 퇴근하고 헬스장에 가요.** I go to the gym every day after work.
비용	cost, expense, charge	**비용이 어느 정도 들까요?** How much will it cost?

Let's review!

Complete the story from Day 42 using the words you just learned.

내 _____ 동생은 _____.

내가 보기에는 귀여운데, 동생은 _____이 너무 _____ 생각한다.

그래서 요즘 살을 _____ 밥을 _____ 한다.

마음은 _____, 굶는 것은 몸에 안 좋다.

그래서 나는 동생에게 _____ 운동을 하라고 말했다.

그리고 _____ _____을 대신 내 주었다.

사촌 동생은 이제 꾸준히 운동을 한다.

Translation

My younger <u>cousin</u> is <u>plump</u>. He looks cute to me, but he thinks <u>he</u> is too <u>fat</u>. So he says that he <u>skips meals</u> to <u>lose</u> weight these days. I <u>understand</u> how he feels, but skipping meals is bad for the body. So I told him to exercise <u>steadily</u>. And I paid for his <u>gym</u> membership <u>fees</u>. My younger cousin works out steadily now.

Crossword Puzzle

			01			
02						
		03				
04				05		
		06				
07						

01 to understand

02 to lose (weight)

03 to gain weight

04 cost, expense, charge

05 to skip[miss] a meal, to starve

06 cousin

07 steadily, consistently

Fill in the blanks with Korean words that matches its English translation.

Word bank	
사촌	굶다
통통하다	이해하다
본인	꾸준히
살찌다	헬스장
빼다	비용

01 oneself

_____

02 to gain weight

_____

03 to understand

_____

04 to be plump, to be chubby

_____

05 gym

_____

Day 43

Day 43

....

Imagine the situation in the story below to remember the ten Korean words in context.

나는 길을 자주 물어본다.

I often ask for directions.

대부분의 **경우** 사람들은 **냉정하게 지나간다**.

In **most cases**, people **pass by coldly**.

그런데 오늘은 달랐다.

But today was different.

신호등에 서 있는 사람에게 길을 물어봤는데 **자세히** 알려 줬다.

I asked a person at the **traffic light** for directions, and she told me the way **in detail**.

그리고 버스에 타기 전, 몇몇 사람이 먼저 타라고 **비켜** 줬다.

And before I got on the bus, some people **stepped aside** to let me get on the bus first.

심지어 버스가 **목적지**에 도착했을 때, **기사**님은 나에게 목적지에 도착했다고 알려 주셨다.

<u>On top of that,</u> when the bus arrived at my <u>destination</u>, the <u>driver</u> informed me that we had arrived.

Let's keep the ball rolling!

Word	Meaning	Example
대부분	most	저는 이 아파트에 사는 사람들 대부분을 알아요. I know most of the people who live in this apartment building.
경우	case, occasion	이런 경우는 처음 봐요. I've never seen a case like this.
냉정하다	to be cold, to be cold-hearted	동생한테 너무 냉정한 거 아니야? Aren't you being too cold to your younger brother/sister?
지나가다	to pass (by), to go (by)	버스가 안 멈추고 그냥 지나갔어요. The bus has just passed by without stopping.
신호등	traffic lights	지금 신호등에 멈춰 있어요. I'm stopped at a traffic light right now.
자세히	in detail	자세히 좀 말해 봐요. Please tell me in detail.

비키다	to step aside	좀 비켜 주세요. Please step aside for me.
심지어	even, on top of that	심지어 같은 동네에 살고 있어요. We even live in the same neighborhood.
목적지	destination	친구랑 이야기하다가 목적지를 지나쳤어요. While talking with my friend, I passed my destination.
기사	driver	매일 같은 버스를 타서 기사님과 친해졌어요. I rode the same bus every day, so I got close to the driver.

Let's review!

Complete the story from Day 43 using the words you just learned.

나는 길을 자주 물어본다.

_____의 ____ 사람들은 _____ _____ .

그런데 오늘은 달랐다.

_____에 서 있는 사람에게 길을 물어봤는데 _____ 알려 줬다.

그리고 버스에 타기 전, 몇몇 사람이 먼저 타라고 ____ 줬다.

_____ 버스가 _____에 도착했을 때, ____님은 나에게 목적지에 도착했다고 알려 주셨다.

Translation

I often ask for directions. In **most cases**, people **pass by coldly**. But today was different. I asked a person at the **traffic light** for directions, and she told me the way **in detail**. And before I got on the bus, some people **stepped aside** to let me get on the bus first. **On top of that,** when the bus arrived at my **destination**, the **driver** informed me that we had arrived.

Word Search – Find 7 words out of the vocabulary you just learned in this chapter.

경	우	나	거	선	차	대
구	하	꽃	자	허	촌	부
지	나	가	다	등	둥	분
예	카	섬	지	어	냉	오
자	묵	기	사	지	정	마
세	적	춤	윤	세	하	코
히	지	숭	비	키	다	림

....

Fill in the blanks with Korean words that matches its English translation.

Word bank	
대부분	자세히
경우	비키다
냉정하다	심지어
지나가다	목적지
신호등	기사

01 even, on top of that   _____

02 case, occasion   _____

03 traffic lights   _____

04 destination   _____

05 to step aside   _____

Day 44

Day 44

Let's warm up!

Imagine the situation in the story below to remember the ten Korean words in context.

떡볶이는 만들기 쉬운 음식이다.

Tteokbokki is an easy food to make.

먼저 냄비에 물을 붓는다.

First, pour water into a pot.

떡, 고추장, 설탕을 같이 넣고 끓인다.

Add rice cakes, red chili paste, and sugar, then bring it to a boil.

그리고 양배추, 양파를 넣는다.

And add cabbage and onion.

나는 치즈도 꼭 넣는다.

I also always add cheese.

이제 재료가 다 익을 때까지 기다린다.

Then wait until the ingredients are cooked.

딱딱한 떡이 부드럽게 되면 다 익은 것이다.

When the hard rice cake becomes soft, it is fully cooked.

그럼 맛있게 먹으면 된다.

Then you can enjoy eating it.

Let's keep the ball rolling!

Word	Meaning	Example
떡볶이	tteokbokki	요즘 떡볶이를 매일 먹고 있어요. These days, I eat tteokbokki every day.
냄비	pot	엄마, 냄비 어디에 있어요? Mom, where is the pot?
붓다	to pour	따뜻한 물 좀 부어 주세요. Please pour some warm water.
고추장	red chili paste	저는 멸치를 고추장에 찍어 먹는 걸 좋아해요. I like to eat anchovies dipped in red chili paste.
끓다	to boil	미역국은 오래 끓일수록 맛있어요. The longer you boil the seaweed soup, the better it tastes.
양배추	cabbage	양배추는 쪄서 먹는 게 가장 맛있어요. Cabbage tastes the best when it's steamed.

| 치즈 | cheese | 치즈 케이크 좋아해요?
Do you like cheesecake? |

| 익다 | to be cooked,
to be done | 고기는 아직 더 익혀야 할 것 같아요.
I think the meat needs to be cooked more. |

| 딱딱하다 | to be hard | 오늘 하루 동안은 딱딱한 거 먹지 마세요.
Don't eat hard foods for today. |

| 부드럽다 | to be soft | 할머니가 드실 수 있는 부드러운 음식이
뭐가 있을까요?
What are some soft foods that my grandmother
can eat? |

Let's review!

Complete the story from Day 44 using the words you just learned.

_____는 만들기 쉬운 음식이다.

먼저 ____에 물을 _____.

떡, _____, 설탕을 같이 넣고 _____.

그리고 _____, 양파를 넣는다.

나는 ____도 꼭 넣는다.

이제 재료가 다 ____ 때까지 기다린다.

_____ 떡이 _____ 되면 다 익은 것이다.

그럼 맛있게 먹으면 된다.

Translation

Tteokbokki is an easy food to make. First, <u>pour</u> water into a <u>pot</u>. Add rice cakes, <u>red chili paste</u>, and sugar, then bring it to a <u>boil</u>. And add <u>cabbage</u> and onion. I also always add <u>cheese</u>. Then wait until the ingredients <u>are cooked</u>. When the <u>hard</u> rice cake becomes <u>soft</u>, it is fully cooked. Then you can enjoy eating it.

Crossword Puzzle

				01		
02					03	
		04				
	05					
			06			
	07					

01 cheese

02 to pour

03 tteokbokki

04 to be cooked, to be done

05 pot

06 to boil

07 to be hard

Fill in the blanks with Korean words that matches its English translation.

Word bank	
떡볶이	양배추
냄비	치즈
붓다	익다
고추장	딱딱하다
끓다	부드럽다

01 cabbage   _____

02 to be soft   _____

03 to be hard   _____

04 red chili paste   _____

05 to pour   _____

Day 45

Let's warm up!

Imagine the situation in the story below to
remember the ten Korean words in context.

내 앞자리 사람은 **향수**를 **심하게 뿌린다**.

The person in front of me <u>sprays</u> <u>perfume</u> <u>excessively</u>.

그 냄새 때문에 **두통**이 생기고, **소화**도 잘 안되는 것
같다.

Because of that smell, I think I got a <u>headache</u> and have trouble
<u>digesting</u>.

향수를 **그만** 뿌리라고 말하고 싶었다.

I wanted to tell her to <u>stop</u> spraying perfume.

하지만 그런 말을 하는 건 **예의**가 아닌 것 같았다.

But I thought it would show a lack of <u>courtesy</u> to say that.

서로 **감정**이 상할 것 같았다.

I thought it would result in hurting each other's <u>feelings</u>.

그래서 그 사람을 **피해서** 내 자리를 다른 곳으로
옮겼다.

So I <u>avoided</u> her and <u>moved</u> my seat to another place.

Let's keep the ball rolling!

Word	Meaning	Example
향수	perfume, cologne	어떤 향수 써요? What kind of perfume do you use?
심하다	to be severe, to be serious, to be excessive	심하게 다치지 않아서 다행이에요. It's fortunate that you didn't get seriously hurt.
뿌리다	to spray, to sprinkle	얼굴에서 20cm 정도 떨어진 거리에서 뿌리세요. Spray at a distance of about 20cm from your face.
두통	headache	두통 때문에 잠을 못 잤어요. I couldn't sleep because of a headache.
소화	digestion, digest	요즘 소화가 잘 안돼요. I'm having trouble with my digestion these days.
그만	no more, stop doing	텔레비전 그만 보고, 책 좀 읽어. Stop watching television and please read a book.

예의	manners, etiquette, courtesy	공공장소에서 시끄럽게 떠드는 건 예의가 아니에요. It's not good manners to talk loudly in public.
감정	feeling(s), emotion(s)	어떤 감정을 느꼈어요? What kind of feelings did you feel?
피하다	to avoid	요즘 경화 씨가 자꾸 절 피하는 것 같아요. I think Kyung-hwa keeps avoiding me these days.
옮기다	to move, to take	우리 창가 자리로 옮길래? Why don't we move to the window seat?

Let's review!

Complete the story from Day 45 using the words you just learned.

내 앞자리 사람은 _____를 _____ _____.

그 냄새 때문에 _____이 생기고, _____도 잘 안되는 것 같다.

향수를 _____ 뿌리라고 말하고 싶었다.

하지만 그런 말을 하는 건 _____가 아닌 것 같았다.

서로 _____이 상할 것 같았다.

그래서 그 사람을 _____ 내 자리를 다른 곳으로 _____.

Translation

The person in front of me <u>sprays</u> <u>perfume</u> <u>excessively</u>. Because of that smell, I think I got a <u>headache</u> and have trouble <u>digesting</u>. I wanted to tell her to <u>stop</u> spraying perfume. But I thought it would show a lack of <u>courtesy</u> to say that. I thought it would result in hurting each other's <u>feelings</u>. So I <u>avoided</u> her and <u>moved</u> my seat to another place.

Word Search – Find 7 words out of the vocabulary you just learned in this chapter.

헝	소	뿌	관	제	통	두
성	회	리	소	열	그	만
심	하	다	울	수	주	자
리	다	제	커	지	두	통
소	시	건	분	피	영	목
화	열	자	감	정	디	향
만	그	화	푸	두	나	수

....

Fill in the blanks with Korean words that matches its English translation.

Word bank	
향수	그만
심하다	예의
뿌리다	감정
두통	피하다
소화	옮기다

01 feeling(s), emotion(s)   _____

02 manners, etiquette, courtesy   _____

03 to avoid   _____

04 to move, to take   _____

05 to spray, to sprinkle   _____

Day 46

⬡ 드디어 ----------------- ⬡

⬡ 초급 -------------------- ⬡

⬡ 중급 -------------------- ⬡

⬡ 학습하다 --------------- ⬡

⬡ 문장 -------------------- ⬡

⬡ 뜻 ----------------------- ⬡

⬡ 가리다 ------------------ ⬡

⬡ 외우다 ------------------ ⬡

⬡ 반복하다 --------------- ⬡

⬡ 점수 -------------------- ⬡

Day 46

Let's warm up!

Imagine the situation in the story below to remember the ten Korean words in context.

드디어 초급 단어 책 공부를 끝냈다.

I **finally** finished studying with a **beginner-level** vocabulary book.

그래서 **중급** 단어 책을 샀다.

So I bought a vocabulary book for the **intermediate level**.

이 책으로는 500개의 단어를 **학습할** 수 있다.

With this book, I can **study** 500 words.

그리고 그 단어들을 사용해서 만든 이야기와 **문장**도 배울 수 있다.

And I can also learn the stories and **sentences** made using these words.

단어를 잘 **외웠는지** 알고 싶으면, 단어의 **뜻**을 **가리고** 확인해 본다.

When I want to know if I **memorized** some words well, I **cover** the **meanings** of the words and check.

이 책을 **반복해서** 공부하면, 한국어 시험에서 좋은 **점수**를 받을 것 같다.

If I study with this book **repeatedly**, I think I will get a good **score** on the Korean language test.

Let's keep the ball rolling!

Word	Meaning	Example
드디어	finally, eventually, at long last	드디어 저도 성인이 됐어요! I have finally become an adult!
초급	beginning level, beginner level	초급 수영반에 등록했어요. I signed up for the beginner-level swimming class.
중급	intermediate level	그 책은 중급 수준의 책인 것 같네요. I think it's an intermediate-level book.
학습하다	to study, to learn	오늘 학습한 내용을 다시 살펴봅시다. Let's check what we learned today.
문장	sentence	마지막 문장을 잘 읽어 보세요. Read the last sentence carefully.
뜻	meaning	아까 한 말 무슨 뜻이에요? What did you mean by what you said earlier?

가리다	to cover, to hide, to conceal	사진 찍을 때 왜 얼굴을 가려? When you take pictures, why do you cover your face?
외우다	to memorize	너는 너희 반 학생들 이름 다 외웠어? Did you memorize all the students' names in your class ?
반복하다	to repeat	나는 같은 실수를 반복하고 싶지 않아. I don't want to repeat the same mistake.
점수	score, grade	저 이번에 시험 점수 많이 올랐어요! My test score went up by a lot this time!

Let's review!

Complete the story from Day 46 using the words you just learned.

_____ _____ 단어 책 공부를 끝냈다.

그래서 _____ 단어 책을 샀다.

이 책으로는 500개의 단어를 _____ 수 있다.

그리고 그 단어들을 사용해서 만든 이야기와 _____도 배울 수 있다.

단어를 잘 _____ 알고 싶으면, 단어의 __을 _____ 확인해 본다.

이 책을 _____ 공부하면, 한국어 시험에서 좋은 _____를 받을 것 같다.

Translation

I **finally** finished studying with a **beginner-level** vocabulary book. So I bought a vocabulary book for the **intermediate level**. With this book, I can **study** 500 words. And I can also learn the stories and **sentences** made using these words. When I want to know if I **memorized** some words well, I **cover** the **meanings** of the words and check. If I study with this book **repeatedly**, I think I will get a good **score** on the Korean language test.

Crossword Puzzle

		01				
	02			03		
04			05			
					06	
	07					

01 beginning level, beginner level

02 intermediate level

03 to study, to learn

04 score, grade

05 to repeat

06 sentence

07 to memorize

Fill in the blanks with Korean words that matches its English translation.

Word bank	
드디어	뜻
초급	가리다
중급	외우다
학습하다	반복하다
문장	점수

01 meaning
_____

02 to study, to learn
_____

03 finally, eventually, at long last
_____

04 to cover, to hide, to conceal
_____

05 to memorize
_____

Day 47

⬡	**목표** ---------------------	⬡
⬡	**이루다** -------------------	⬡
⬡	**최선** ---------------------	⬡
⬡	**상황** ---------------------	⬡
⬡	**조건** ---------------------	⬡
⬡	**가난하다** -----------------	⬡
⬡	**뛰어나다** -----------------	⬡
⬡	**능력** ---------------------	⬡
⬡	**긍정적** -------------------	⬡
⬡	**태도** ---------------------	⬡

Day 47

Let's warm up!

....

Imagine the situation in the story below to remember the ten Korean words in context.

목표를 이루지 못하면 사람들은 실패했다고 생각한다.
When you cannot **achieve** a **goal**, people think you have failed.

하지만 최선을 다했으면 그것은 실패가 아니다.
But if you **did your best**, it is not a failure.

상황이나 조건이 안 좋아도 괜찮다.
It is okay even if the **situation** or **conditions** are bad.

가난해도 괜찮다.
It is okay if you are **poor**.

뛰어난 능력이 없어도 괜찮다.
It is okay if you do not have **outstanding abilities**.

항상 긍정적인 태도를 가지면 성공할 수 있을 것이다.
If you always have a **positive attitude**, you will be able to succeed.

Let's keep the ball rolling!

Word	Meaning	Example
목표	goal, aim	내 목표는 한국어로 편지를 쓰는 거야. My goal is to write a letter in Korean.
이루다	to achieve	드디어 내 꿈을 이루었어! I finally achieved my dream!
최선	(doing) one's best	난 최선을 다했으니까 후회 없어. I did my best, so I have no regrets.
상황	situation, circumstance	상황이 점점 심각해지고 있는 것 같습니다. The situation seems to be getting worse and worse.
조건	condition	저 선수는 신체적인 조건이 정말 좋죠. The physical condition of that player is really good.
가난하다	to be poor	그때는 너무 가난해서 밥도 제대로 못 먹고 살았어. At that time, I was so poor that I couldn't even eat properly.

뛰어나다	to be excellent, to be outstanding	우리 과장님은 기억력이 진짜 뛰어나신 것 같아. I think my manager is excellent at remembering things.
능력	ability, capacity	인간의 능력에는 한계가 있습니다. There is a limit to human abilities.
긍정적	positive, affirmative	긍정적인 사람들 옆에 있으면 기분이 좋아. When I'm around positive people, I feel good.
태도	attitude	학생들이 진지한 태도로 수업을 듣기 시작했어요. The students began to take the class with a serious attitude.

Let's review!

Complete the story from Day 47 using the words you just learned.

_____를 _____ 못하면 사람들은 실패했다고 생각한다.

하지만 _____을 다했으면 그것은 실패가 아니다.

_____이나 _____이 안 좋아도 괜찮다.

_____ 괜찮다.

_____ _____이 없어도 괜찮다.

항상 _____ _____를 가지면 성공할 수 있을 것이다.

Translation

When you cannot <u>achieve</u> a <u>goal</u>, people think you have failed. But if you <u>did your best</u>, it is not a failure. It is okay if the <u>situation</u> or <u>conditions</u> are bad. It is okay if you are <u>poor</u>. It is okay even if you do not have <u>outstanding</u> <u>abilities</u>. If you always have a <u>positive</u> <u>attitude</u>, you will be able to succeed.

Word Search - Find 7 words out of the vocabulary you just learned in this chapter.

뛰	어	나	다	더	꿈	능
편	저	한	타	가	디	력
쓰	태	도	계	난	루	표
흐	심	진	이	하	한	먹
최	난	이	루	다	분	테
선	각	선	체	저	궁	업
목	들	생	상	황	수	한

. . . .

Fill in the blanks with Korean words that matches its English translation.

Word bank	
목표	가난하다
이루다	뛰어나다
최선	능력
상황	긍정적
조건	태도

01 condition   _____

02 positive, affirmative   _____

03 to achieve   _____

04 goal, aim   _____

05 to be poor   _____

Day 48

출근하다 ----------------

선배 --------------------

인쇄하다 ----------------

파일 --------------------

삭제하다 ----------------

프린터 ------------------

한참 --------------------

완전히 ------------------

포기하다 ----------------

모니터 ------------------

Day 48

Let's warm up!

....

Imagine the situation in the story below to remember the ten Korean words in context.

오늘은 출근하자마자 실수를 많이 했다.

Not long after I <u>went to work</u> today, I made many mistakes.

먼저, **선배**가 **인쇄해** 놓으라고 한 **파일**을 **삭제해** 버렸다.

First, I <u>deleted</u> the <u>file</u> that my <u>senior</u> told me to <u>print</u>.

그리고 **프린터**도 고장을 냈다.

And I also broke the <u>printer</u>.

한참 동안 고치려고 해 봤는데 계속 안 됐다.

I tried to fix it <u>for a long time</u>, but it did not work.

완전히 고장이 난 것이었다.

It was <u>completely</u> out of order.

포기하고 자리에 갔는데 **모니터**도 고장이 나 있었다.

I <u>gave up</u> and went to my seat, but the <u>monitor</u> was also broken.

이제 어떡하지?

What should I do now?

Let's keep the ball rolling!

Word	Meaning	Example
출근하다	to go to work	보통 몇 시에 출근해요? What time do you usually go to work?
선배	superior, senior	그 남자가 회사에서 나보다 2년 선배야. He is two years my senior at my company.
인쇄하다	to print	인쇄하려고 하는데 인쇄기가 안 되네요. I'm trying to print, but the printer isn't working.
파일	file	그 파일 나한테 보내 줄 수 있어? Can you send me the file?
삭제하다	to delete	나 실수로 네가 보낸 사진들 삭제해 버렸어. I accidentally deleted the pictures you sent me.
프린터	printer	사무실에 새 프린터가 설치되었습니다. A new printer has been installed in our office.

| 한참 | for a long time, for a while | 여기서 집까지 걸어가면 시간이 한참 걸려. |
| | | If you walk home from here, it will take a long time. |

| 완전히 | completely, absolutely | 버스가 완전히 멈추면 내리세요. |
| | | Get off when the bus stops completely. |

| 포기하다 | to give up | 포기하지 말고 꾸준히 공부해 보세요. |
| | | Don't give up and continue to study. |

| 모니터 | monitor | 이 모니터는 텔레비전으로도 쓸 수 있고 컴퓨터로도 쓸 수 있어요. |
| | | This monitor can be used as a television as well as a computer. |

Let's review!

Complete the story from Day 48 using the words you just learned.

오늘은 ＿＿＿＿＿＿＿＿ 실수를 많이 했다.

먼저, ＿＿＿가 ＿＿＿＿ 놓으라고 한 ＿＿＿을 ＿＿＿＿ 버렸다.

그리고 ＿＿＿＿도 고장을 냈다.

＿＿＿ 동안 고치려고 해 봤는데 계속 안 됐다.

＿＿＿＿ 고장이 난 것이었다.

＿＿＿＿＿ 자리에 갔는데 ＿＿＿＿도 고장이 나 있었다.

이제 어떡하지?

Translation

Not long after I **went to work** today, I made many mistakes. First, I **deleted** the **file** that my **senior** told me to **print**. And I also broke the **printer**. I tried to fix it **for a long time**, but it did not work. It was **completely** out of order. I **gave up** and went to my seat, but the **monitor** was also broken. What should I do now?

Crossword Puzzle

		01		02		
						03
04						
			05			
	06					
			07			

01 to print

02 for a long time, for a while

03 printer

04 to go to work

05 monitor

06 superior, senior

07 completely, absolutely

Fill in the blanks with Korean words that matches its English translation.

Word bank	
출근하다	프린터
선배	한참
인쇄하다	완전히
파일	포기하다
삭제하다	모니터

01 file _____

02 completely, absolutely _____

03 to delete _____

04 to give up _____

05 to print _____

Day 49

Day 49

Let's warm up!

Imagine the situation in the story below to
remember the ten Korean words in context.

계획을 **세울** 때는 누구나 계획을 **그대로 지킬** 수
있다고 생각한다.

When people **make** a plan, everyone thinks they can **keep** their
plan **as it is**.

하지만 **업무**를 **진행해** 보면 **예상하지** 못한 일이
생긴다.

However, when you **proceed** with the **work**, something that you
did not **expect** occurs.

그러니까 계획을 세울 때는 쉬는 시간도 **포함해서**
여유롭게 세워야 한다.

So when you make a plan, you need to make a plan **flexibly**,
including some time to rest.

그리고 처음부터 할 수 있는 **만큼**의 업무만 **맡는** 것도
중요하다.

And it is also important to **take on** only **as much** work **as** you can
do from the beginning.

그러지 않으면, 짧은 시간에 너무 많은 양의 업무를 해야 할
것이다.

If not, you will have to do too much work in a short time.

Let's keep the ball rolling!

Word	Meaning	Example
세우다	to make (plan), to set up	이번 주 여행 계획은 내가 세울게. I'll make plans for the trip this week.
그대로	as it is, the way it is	아무것도 만지지 말고 그대로 둬. Don't touch anything and leave everything just as it is.
지키다	to keep	나랑 한 약속 진짜 지킬 거지? Will you keep your promise with me for sure?
업무	work, job	업무가 너무 많아서 요즘 정말 바빠. I have so much work, so I'm really busy these days.
진행하다	to progress, to proceed, to do something	그 프로젝트는 어떻게 진행되고 있어요? How is the project progressing?
예상하다	to expect	오늘 경기에서 누가 이길 거라고 예상하십니까? Who do you expect will win the game today?

포함하다	to include	**음료수 포함해서 총 3만 원입니다.** It's 30,000 won including drinks.
여유롭다	to be relaxed, to be flexible, to not be busy or hastened	**이 카페는 분위기가 여유로워서 좋아.** I like this cafe because it has a relaxed atmosphere.
만큼	as ... as	**너 먹고 싶은 만큼 먹어.** Eat as much as you want to eat.
맡다	to take on, to undertake	**제가 맡은 업무는 다 했어요.** I've completed all the work I took on.

Let's review!

Complete the story from Day 49 using the words you just learned.

계획을 _____ 때는 누구나 계획을 _____ _____ 수 있다고 생각한다.

하지만 _____를 _____ 보면 _____ 못한 일이 생긴다.

그러니까 계획을 세울 때는 쉬는 시간도 _____ _____ 세워야 한다.

그리고 처음부터 할 수 있는 _____의 업무만 _____ 것도 중요하다.

그러지 않으면, 짧은 시간에 너무 많은 양의 업무를 해야 할 것이다.

Translation

When people **make** a plan, everyone thinks they can **keep** their plan **as it is**. However, when you **proceed** with the **work**, something that you did not **expect** occurs. So when you make a plan, you need to make a plan **flexibly**, **including** some time to rest. And it is also important to **take on** only **as much** work **as** you can do from the beginning. If not, you will have to do too much work in a short time.

Word Search - Find 7 words out of the vocabulary you just learned in this chapter.

그	대	로	계	세	포	획
번	아	주	이	게	함	우
업	무	모	예	상	하	다
경	분	고	만	업	다	지
여	고	만	큼	상	로	믈
필	류	다	더	지	키	다
진	행	하	다	키	보	볼

Fill in the blanks with Korean words that matches its English translation.

Word bank	
세우다	예상하다
그대로	포함하다
지키다	여유롭다
업무	만큼
진행하다	맡다

01 to make (plan), to set up

_____

02 to be relaxed, to be flexible,
to not be busy or hastened

_____

03 to expect

_____

04 as it is, the way it is

_____

05 to take on, to undertake

_____

Day 50

⬡ **경제** ------------------------ ⬡

⬡ **아끼다** ---------------------- ⬡

⬡ **월급** ------------------------ ⬡

⬡ **전부** ------------------------ ⬡

⬡ **일부** ------------------------ ⬡

⬡ **잔돈** ------------------------ ⬡

⬡ **모으다** ---------------------- ⬡

⬡ **계좌** ------------------------ ⬡

⬡ **총** -------------------------- ⬡

⬡ **금액** ------------------------ ⬡

Day 50

Let's warm up!

Imagine the situation in the story below to remember the ten Korean words in context.

요즘 **경제** 상황이 좋지 않다.

These days the **economic** situation is not good.

돈을 **아끼면** 좋을 것 같았다.

I thought it would be a good idea to **save** money.

그래서 **월급**을 받으면 거의 **전부** 저축하고 **일부**만 썼다.

So when I received my **salary**, I saved almost **all** of it and spent only a **part** of it.

잔돈도 전부 **모았다**.

I also **gathered** all the **small change**.

그리고 오늘 **계좌**에 있는 **총 금액**을 확인했다.

And today, I checked the **total** amount of **money** in my **account**.

생각보다 많은 금액이 있었다. 기분이 좋았다.

There was more money than I had thought. It felt good.

Let's keep the ball rolling!

Word	Meaning	Example
경제	economy	우리나라 경제가 점점 발전하고 있습니다. Our country's economy is developing more and more.
아끼다	to save	용돈 아껴서 가방 살 거야. I'm going to save my pocket money and buy a bag.
월급	salary	이번 달 월급은 8일에 입금될 거예요. This month's salary will be deposited on the 8th of this month.
전부	all	내 모든 사랑을 전부 너한테 줄 거야. I'll give all of my love to you.
일부	part	서울 일부 지역은 아직 공사 중입니다. Some parts of Seoul are still under construction.
잔돈	small change	잔돈 여기 있습니다. Here's your change.

모으다	to gather	돈 모아서 한국으로 여행 갈 거야. I'll save money and travel to Korea.
계좌	account	제 계좌로 5천 원씩 보내 주세요. Please send five thousand won each to my account.
총	total	대회에 참가하는 선수는 총 3백 명입니다. There are a total of three hundred athletes participating in the competition.
금액	money	이번 달에 지불할 금액은 4만 원입니다. The amount you should pay this month is forty thousand won.

Let's review!

Complete the story from Day 50 using the words you just learned.

요즘 _____ 상황이 좋지 않다.

돈을 _____ 좋을 것 같았다.

그래서 _____을 받으면 거의 _____ 저축하고 _____만 썼다.

_____도 전부 _____.

그리고 오늘 _____에 있는 __ _____을 확인했다.

생각보다 많은 금액이 있었다. 기분이 좋았다.

Translation

These days the <u>economic</u> situation is not good. I thought it would be a good idea to <u>save</u> money. So when I received my <u>salary</u>, I saved almost <u>all</u> of it and spent only a <u>part</u> of it. I also <u>gathered</u> all the <u>small change</u>. And today, I checked the <u>total</u> amount of <u>money</u> in my <u>account</u>. There was more money than I had thought. It felt good.

Crossword Puzzle

	01			02		
03					04	
			05			
06				07		

01 part

02 salary

03 all

04 to save

05 to gather

06 money

07 economy

Fill in the blanks with Korean words that matches its English translation.

Word bank	
경제	잔돈
아끼다	모으다
월급	계좌
전부	총
일부	금액

01 to save   _____

02 total   _____

03 small change   _____

04 account   _____

05 salary   _____

01 Choose the word that is <u>not</u> an edible item.

    a. 양배추   **b.** 새우   **c.** 모래   **d.** 떡볶이

02 Choose the word that is related to banks.

    a. 향수   **b.** 계좌   **c.** 사촌   **d.** 헬스장

03 What is the Korean word for the item in the picture? _____

04 Write down the past form of the descriptive verb "부드럽다". _____

05 Choose the word that you can see.

    a. 목표   **b.** 냄비   **c.** 공기   **d.** 두통

06 Choose the pair of actions and tools which are <u>not</u> matched correctly.
   a. 인쇄하다 - 프린터   **b.** 뿌리다 - 향수
   c. 학습하다 - 책   **d.** 지나가다 - 냄비

07 Write the character that can fit in all of the blanks. _____

해수욕____	문____	고추____
= beach	= sentence	= red chili paste

08 Which of the following does <u>not</u> become a verb if you attach -하다?
   a. 아끼   **b.** 반복   **c.** 삭제   **d.** 포기

09 How do you say "salary" in Korean? _____

10 What is the antonym of 일부? _____

Fill in the blanks using the words that you learned in Day 41 - Day 50.

11 햇빛이 너무 _____ 눈을 못 뜨겠어요.
    = The sun is too dazzling, so I can't open my eyes.

12 저는 _____(이)랑 별로 안 친해요.
    = I'm not very close with my cousin.

13 _____ 좀 말해 봐요.
    = Please tell me in detail.

14 미역국은 오래 _____ 맛있어요.
    = The longer you boil the seaweed soup, the better it tastes.

15 텔레비전 _____ 보고, 책 좀 읽어.
    = Stop watching television and please read a book.

16 오늘 _____ 내용을 다시 살펴봅시다.
    = Let's check what we learned today.

17 난 _____을/를 다했으니까 후회 없어.

= I did my best, so I have no regrets.

18 _____ 말고 꾸준히 공부해 보세요.

= Don't give up and continue to study.

19 나랑 한 약속 진짜 _____ 거지?

= Will you keep your promise with me for sure?

20 대회에 참가하는 선수는 _____ 3백 명입니다.

= There are a total of three hundred athletes participating in the competition.

QUIZ
DAY 41-50

ANSWERS ◈

INDEX ◈

ANSWERS

Day 01
page 026

Word Search

북	소	하	평	느	료	**후**
치	언	준	곤	민	**외**	**식**
취	**소**	**하**	**다**	담	고	타
양	식	버	**양**	란	**마**	**늘**
편	러	골	**하**	많	싶	잠
달	**콤**	**하**	**다**	언	즙	방
안	프	떠	조	**볶**	**다**	쁘

Fill in the blanks

01 야경
02 후식
03 훌륭하다
04 선약
05 취소하다

Day 02
page 032

Crossword Puzzle

	발				해
	급				외
		제			여
		안		일	행
출	국	하	다	정	
		다			
				전	통

Fill in the blanks

01 싸다
02 비자
03 체험
04 발급
05 제안하다

Day 03
page 038

Word Search

지	원	최	좌	등	할	늦
야	부	방	앞	록	쉬	말
두	머	법	역	증	연	표
감	폰	발	접	선	면	작
동	휴	센	터	쇼	존	성
하	기	거	수	멘	화	하
다	맛	로	따	라	오	다

Fill in the blanks

01 유학생
02 자기
03 작성하다
04 대하다
05 방법

Day 04
page 044

Crossword Puzzle

공		제	대	로		마
연						침
	관			예		
	객			매		
		집	중	하	다	
				다		
떠	들	다				

Fill in the blanks

01 용돈
02 마침
03 제대로
04 아쉽다
05 감상하다

Day 05
page 050

Word Search

두	추	모	도	충	분	히
화	차	이	중	갑	디	경
토	져	다	기	결	저	초
직	당	깝	차	정	획	운
나	휴	반	대	하	다	국
회	교	출	예	다	역	서
의	견	화	혜	다	방	향

Fill in the blanks

01 찬성하다
02 선택하다
03 방향
04 만족하다
05 의견

Day 06

page 056

Crossword Puzzle

	일	기				사
						실
추			직	장		
억						
		역	할		키	
					우	
		노	력	하	다	

Fill in the blanks

01 외롭다
02 부모
03 키우다
04 가정
05 역할

Day 07

page 062

Word Search

안	기	얼	손	여	하	공
에	대	터	좌	석	지	간
매	하	가	새	사	라	지
펴	다	울	굴	풍	경	요
우	조	무	즘	활	생	막
앞	뒤	미	건	조	하	다
객	공	요	규	죄	해	텃

Fill in the blanks

01 공간
02 등
03 창밖
04 어지럽다
05 좌석

Day 08

page 068

Crossword Puzzle

반	말				
팔				서	
		마	음	대	로
굉	장	히		낯	
				설	
		자	유	롭	다

Fill in the blanks

01 슬리퍼
02 익숙하다
03 마음대로
04 서로
05 별명

Day 09

page 074

page 074

Word Search

면	**접**	다	생	**대**	민	각
료	완	해	**발**	**표**	부	생
쥐	니	소	봉	롯	인	첩
평	**가**	히	**방**	**해**	**하**	**다**
감	본	땡	경	**결**	평	오
접	**인**	**생**	하	**하**	표	보
어	험	규	람	**다**	늦	승

Fill in the blanks

01 버릇
02 대표
03 늦잠
04 평가
05 지각하다

Day 10

page 080

page 080

Crossword Puzzle

		상		꾸	미	다
		상				
		하		정		조
멋	지	다		신		카
				없		
				다		
장	난	감			직	접

Fill in the blanks

01 인형
02 꾸미다
03 서투르다
04 풍선
05 직접

QUIZ Day 01-10

page 081~084

page 081~084

01 b		11	외식
02 일		12	일행
03 c		13	출국하니까
04 반대하다		14	볶은
05 a		15	마침
06 c		16	의견
07 d		17	선약
08 로		18	외롭지
09 풍선		19	어지러우면
10 b		20	굉장히

Day 11

page 090

Word Search

잠	세	**물**	**론**	잔	소	**부**
성	혜	절	라	하	린	**럽**
격	장	럽	**단**	**점**	대	**다**
지	물	**활**	동	격	샤	구
요	현	**발**	겨	론	**거**	소
겸	**손**	**하**	**다**	쇼	**절**	데
부	점	**다**	지	으	머	라

Fill in the blanks

01 부족하다
02 거절
03 장점
04 물론
05 들어주다

Day 12

page 096

Crossword Puzzle

				피	**부**
	머	**리**	**카**	**락**	
하				**여**	
품		**빠**		**드**	
		지		**름**	
	졸	**리**	**다**		**피**
					로

Fill in the blanks

01 푹
02 점점
03 변화
04 하품
05 졸리다

Day 13

page 102

Word Search

가	더	**심**	**다**	은	**야**	라
지	경	소	추	여	**외**	**막**
화	**분**	다	동	**피**	헌	**안**
중	람	진	섬	**다**	배	**네**
랫	**장**	**마**	화	경	란	**실**
바	머	욱	다	예	다	**내**
차	**오**	**랫**	**동**	**안**	희	**마**

Fill in the blanks

01 가꾸다
02 막다
03 화분
04 오랫동안
05 베란다

Day 14
page 108

Crossword Puzzle

전			마	치	다
날		회	식		
	보			겨	우
	고				
	서		기	억	나	다
종					
일					

Fill in the blanks

01 기억나다
02 꽤
03 겨우
04 야근하다
05 제출하다

Day 15
page 114

Word Search

주	나	법	쏟	다	묻	등
걸	턱	자	솔	후	밟	늘
레	도	부	러	지	다	이
미	솔	희	치	전	단	출
웅	탁	자	대	나	따	묻
동	소	레	고	강	증	다
이	고	차	다	비	부	저

Fill in the blanks

01 엉덩이
02 부러지다
03 뼈
04 밟다
05 쏟다

Day 16
page 120

Crossword Puzzle

		닭			학
돌	보	다		누	원
				르	
주	방			다	
				미	술
	도	움			

Fill in the blanks

01 주방
02 연주하다
03 누르다
04 손자
05 악기

Day 17
page 126

Word Search

소	벌	금	다	저	허	구
당	희	초	나	도	다	하
밤	개	후	천	둥	현	다
새	윤	루	동	소	두	지
황	지	다	고	당	장	추
구	망	연	항	숭	다	윤
멍	혜	경	당	황	하	다

Fill in the blanks

01 번개
02 스타킹
03 구하다
04 구멍
05 미끄럽다

Day 18
page 132

Crossword Puzzle

서	랍					
		동	아	리		축
						제
젊				우		
다				연		연
				히		기
		회	장			

Fill in the blanks

01 정리하다
02 신입생
03 축제
04 촬영하다
05 서랍

Day 19
page 138

Word Search

역	하	두	치	가	약	간
아	결	삼	과	랗	건	심
빈	심	다	노	어	소	미
우	하	역	미	루	다	궁
썩	다	지	라	제	경	루
어	해	깔	다	로	습	권
창	훨	씬	간	은	관	보

Fill in the blanks

01 습관
02 깔끔하다
03 썩다
04 창피하다
05 노랗다

Day 20
page 144

Crossword Puzzle

	온	몸		빨		
				갛		
해				다		사
산		국	물			라
물						지
	증			가	렵	다
	상					

Fill in the blanks

01 다행히
02 기침
03 온몸
04 증상
05 알레르기

QUIZ Day 11-20
page 145~148

01 c
02 d
03 서랍
04 c
05 단점
06 b
07 a
08 c
09 b
10 d

11 활발한
12 여드름
13 가꾸는
14 겨우
15 차지
16 학원
17 구멍
18 정리하세요
19 훨씬
20 다행히

Day 21
page 154

Word Search

동	답	치	고	구	고	민
료	가	계	생	별	치	불
도	언	곤	란	하	다	회
늘	초	다	인	친	때	료
사	대	상	불	만	허	지
희	우	소	고	서	포	코
첫	인	상	점	곤	표	정

Fill in the blanks

01 불만
02 상담
03 첫인상
04 조언하다
05 평소

Day 22

page 160

Crossword Puzzle

		가				
딱		습		검		
		기		색		
청	소	기		색		
				하		제
	판	매	하	다		품
			무	료		

Fill in the blanks

01 할인
02 가습기
03 환불
04 제품
05 퍼센트

Day 23

page 166

Word Search

이	상	득	받	트	던	모
추	매	저	회	메	껴	자
등	사	산	피	뉴	담	라
석	문	선	마	판	찍	다
커	햄	버	거	물	어	서
남	다	주	좋	세	모	희
마	튀	가	득	케	봉	지

Fill in the blanks

01 매주
02 모자라다
03 세트
04 남다
05 케첩

Day 24

page 172

Crossword Puzzle

		얇				
자	르	다		단		
				추		
	꼬		완			
	리		성		세	상
			하			
			다		가	위

Fill in the blanks

01 동그랗다
02 완성하다
03 가위
04 재활용하다
05 끈

Day 25
page 178

Word Search

광	고	얼	교	남	보	볼
학	마	집	골	**게**	**시**	**판**
조	야	**목**	푸	하	회	성
구	고	**록**	대	참	급	숭
기	통	줍	**참**	**가**	**하**	**다**
빠	전	혜	파	모	**다**	게
모	**집**	**불**	**총**	**신**	**청**	**서**

Fill in the blanks

01 볼링
02 참가하다
03 목록
04 선수
05 골프

Day 26
page 184

Crossword Puzzle

뚜			상	하	다
껑		보			
		관		만	약
		하			
	덮	다		이	
				미	
음	식	물			

Fill in the blanks

01 녹다
02 얼다
03 만약
04 두다
05 음식물

Day 27
page 190

Word Search

상	음	파	**자**	션	랑	**상**
나	다	라	**랑**	본	감	**태**
자	**튼**	**튼**	**하**	**다**	단	책
거	버	태	**다**	수	**유**	어
가	**죽**	튼	상	죽	**행**	삼
희	패	유	츠	팔	**하**	미
파	**랑**	**다**	티	**검**	**다**	셔

Fill in the blanks

01 튼튼하다
02 살펴보다
03 자랑하다
04 패션
05 셔츠

Day 28

page 196

Crossword Puzzle

	교				좌	
	통			우	회	전
	사				전	
신	고	하	다			
				인		
				도	로	
깨	지	다				

Fill in the blanks

01 살짝
02 깨지다
03 맞은편
04 큰길
05 교통사고

Day 29

page 202

Word Search

보	호	하	다	야	새	심
수	시	케	재	텔	란	각
가	것	그	계	타	바	하
전	장	냥	자	오	냉	다
제	도	력	전	중	마	미
품	보	쉬	호	고	장	서
사	새	롭	다	염	리	기

Fill in the blanks

01 양
02 심각하다
03 보호하다
04 자연
05 기사

Day 30

page 208

Crossword Puzzle

		등			놀	
		록			이	
		금			공	
결	국				원	
		학	과			놓
	기					치
	업		합	격	하	다

Fill in the blanks

01 등
02 결국
03 입학시험
04 합격하다
05 늘

QUIZ Day 21-30

page 209~212

01	c	11	표정
02	b	12	평소
03	가위	13	검색해
04	d	14	봉지
05	녹다	15	상했으니까
06	b	16	살짝
07	중고	17	튼튼해서
08	자	18	기업
09	b	19	놀이공원
10	c	20	무료

Day 31

page 218

Word Search

꾁	넷	지	희	**사**	이	교
경	**자**	**꾸**	우	**과**	수	혼
도	고	종	경	**하**	마	나
얼	효	스	**뺏**	**다**	과	다
른	인	하	해	준	얼	현
학	볼	안	우	**막**	**내**	소
도	**망**	**가**	**다**	나	드	연

Fill in the blanks

01 꽉
02 사과하다
03 화해하다
04 멍
05 뺏다

Day 32

page 224

Crossword Puzzle

Fill in the blanks

01 역시
02 굽다
03 몰래
04 귀찮다
05 숨다

354

Day 33
page 230

page 230

Word Search

석	**체**	**력**	암	**손**	넘
경	략	작	야	더	**목**	서
스	**트**	**레**	**칭**	대	효	**적**
진	인	다	호	**발**	애	**어**
서	트	레	쓰	**목**	서	**도**
한	**동**	**안**	연	혜	**근**	**록**
윤	수	냐	욱	용	**육**	숭

(위 표는 6칸 기준으로 정렬)

Fill in the blanks

01 관리하다
02 스트레칭
03 예방하다
04 안전하다
05 근육

Day 34
page 236

Crossword Puzzle

	경	기		행		
				사		
올	림	픽				
				월	드	컵
경	험					
			사			
			인		통	역

Fill in the blanks

01 입국하다
02 통역
03 추천
04 경기
05 감독

Day 35
page 242

Word Search

알	기	희	**원**	**룸**	율	잔
학	구	완	세	윤	광	세
기	연	텅	장	태	소	시
영	**전**	훈	예	**계**	**약**	지
월	**세**	누	라	역	보	모
래	사	승	**확**	**인**	**하**	**다**
매	**달**	수	언	효	진	은

Fill in the blanks

01 저축하다
02 확인하다
03 계약
04 주변
05 통장

Day 36
page 248

Crossword Puzzle

햇					외	
볕		떨			투	
		어				
		지		챙	기	다
강	하	다				
			기	온		
예	정					

Fill in the blanks

01 전국적
02 챙기다
03 전하다
04 외출하다
05 햇볕

Day 37
page 254

Word Search

하	김	니	분	명	히	정
락	원	막	선	빼	엘	바
헤	피	선	없	이	옷	닥
진	스	우	먹	빈	효	통
윤	다	니	재	아	만	현
사	호	후	하	다	지	영
옷	장	욱	용	끊	다	규

Fill in the blanks

01 막
02 만지다
03 허락
04 없이
05 후회하다

Day 38
page 260

Crossword Puzzle

	사	업	가			
기				부	자	
계						실
	일	상	생	활		제
아	이	디	어			
			관	찰	하	다

Fill in the blanks

01 떠오르다
02 실제
03 연구하다
04 발명하다
05 관찰하다

Day 39
page 266

Word Search

양	**념**	져	**고**	갱	**특**	**징**
최	영	텍	**객**	조	스	턱
입	**맛**	하	귀	좌	**인**	음
효	턱	랩	카	요	**스**	봅
멋	**재**	폰	마	학	**턴**	방
네	**료**	예	세	성	**트**	현
이	다	**기**	**르**	**다**	훈	박

Fill in the blanks

01 입맛
02 지역
03 질
04 재료
05 쌀

Day 40
page 272

Crossword Puzzle

Fill in the blanks

01 냉방
02 달다
03 설명서
04 틀다
05 고생하다

QUIZ Day 31-40
page 273~276

01 a
02 b
03 c
04 사인
05 d
06 d
07 a
08 c
09 d
10 b

11 멍
12 숨고
13 관리해야
14 입국할
15 학기
16 강하게
17 없이
18 연구하고
19 고객
20 고생한

Day 41
page 282

Word Search

지	먼	해	수	욕	장	호
실	컷	코	세	우	훤	연
준	화	다	영	환	하	다
모	경	순	싱	선	자	요
래	마	범	싱	재	렴	아
수	존	성	하	혜	공	호
눈	부	시	다	숙	기	강

Fill in the blanks

01 싱싱하다
02 저렴하다
03 먼지
04 새우
05 공기

Day 42
page 288

Crossword Puzzle

		이	해	하	다
빼	다				
		살	찌	다	
	비				굶
	용		사	촌	다
	꾸	준	히		

Fill in the blanks

01 본인
02 살찌다
03 이해하다
04 통통하다
05 헬스장

Day 43
page 294

Word Search

경	우	나	거	선	차	대
구	하	꽃	자	허	촌	부
지	나	가	다	등	둥	분
예	카	섬	지	어	냉	오
자	묵	기	사	지	정	마
세	적	춤	윤	세	하	코
히	지	숭	비	키	다	림

Fill in the blanks

01 심지어
02 경우
03 신호등
04 목적지
05 비키다

Day 44

page 300

Crossword Puzzle

				치	즈
붓	다				떡
		익	다		볶
	냄				이
	비		끓	다	
	딱	딱	하	다	

Fill in the blanks

01 양배추
02 부드럽다
03 딱딱하다
04 고추장
05 붓다

Day 45

page 306

Word Search

형	소	뿌	관	제	통	두
성	회	리	소	열	그	만
심	하	다	울	수	주	자
리	다	제	커	지	두	통
소	시	건	분	피	영	목
화	열	자	감	정	디	향
만	그	화	푸	두	나	수

Fill in the blanks

01 감정
02 예의
03 피하다
04 옮기다
05 뿌리다

Day 46

page 312

Crossword Puzzle

		초			
	중	급		학	
				습	
점	수		반	하	
			복	다	
			하		문
	외	우	다		장

Fill in the blanks

01 뜻
02 학습하다
03 드디어
04 가리다
05 외우다

Day 47

page 318

Word Search

뛰	어	나	다	더	꿈	능
편	자	한	타	가	디	력
쓰	태	도	계	난	루	표
흐	심	진	이	하	한	먹
최	난	이	루	다	분	테
선	각	선	체	저	궁	업
목	들	생	상	황	수	한

Fill in the blanks

01 조건
02 긍정적
03 이루다
04 목표
05 가난하다

Day 48

page 324

Crossword Puzzle

		인		한	참	
		쇄				프
출	근	하	다			린
		다		모	니	터
		선				
		배		완	전	히

Fill in the blanks

01 파일
02 완전히
03 삭제하다
04 포기하다
05 인쇄하다

Day 49

page 330

Word Search

그	대	로	계	세	포	획
번	아	주	이	게	함	우
업	무	모	예	상	하	다
경	분	고	만	업	다	지
여	고	만	큼	상	로	믈
필	류	다	더	지	키	다
진	행	하	다	키	보	볼

Fill in the blanks

01 세우다
02 여유롭다
03 예상하다
04 그대로
05 맡다

Day 50

page 336

Crossword Puzzle

	일		월	
전	부		급	아
				끼
			모 으	다
	금	액		경
				제

Fill in the blanks

01　아끼다
02　총
03　잔돈
04　계좌
05　월급

QUIZ Day 41-50

page 337~340

01	c	11	눈부셔서
02	b	12	사촌
03	신호등	13	자세히
04	부드러웠다	14	끓일수록
05	b	15	그만
06	d	16	학습한
07	장	17	최선
08	a	18	포기하지
09	월급	19	지킬
10	전부	20	총

INDEX   Listed in Korean dictionary order

ㅁ

ㅎ

열심히 공부한 여러분! 정말 수고하셨습니다.
You've just completed your 50-day journey
to improve your Korean vocabulary skills. Well done!

Continue learning more with our video
and audio lessons by visiting our website
at *https://talktomeinkorean.com*!

TTMIK Book Audio App

Download our app **TTMIK: Audio** to listen to all the audio and video tracks from our book conveniently on your phone! The app is available for free on both iOS and Android. Search for **TTMIK: Audio** in your app store.